Language, Community and the State

Dennis Ager

EXETER, ENGLAND

First Published in 1997 by
Intellect Books
EFAE, Earl Richards Road North, Exeter EX2 6AS, UK

Series editor:	Keith Cameron
Production:	Robin Beecroft
Copy editor:	Siobhan Prendergast
Cover illustration:	Myles Hunt

British Library Cataloguing in Publication Data Available

ISBN 1-871516-94-3

Printed and bound in Great Britain by Cromwell Press, Wiltshire

Contents

Preface

Languages, individuals and communities

In this book we shall be examining different ways in which linguists, political scientists and sociologists look at Europe and her languages. Linguists deal mainly with language: firstly with language as a system (often an abstract one quite unlike any actual language) and then with individual languages and the ways they relate both to such a system and also to their users, whether as individuals or in communities.

Political scientists study the ways in which communities structure and control the management of their affairs, and how they govern themselves. They are concerned with language, if at all, both as an object of political policy and also as a weapon in the construction, dissemination and implementation of policy. Sociologists examine relationships within society, and particularly look at why and how groups and communities are formed. Their concern with language is to investigate language use by social groups, social attitudes towards language and the role of language in symbolising, cementing or destroying links within or between communities. All three disciplines study both the historical (diachronic) and the contemporary (synchronic) value of their interests; in different ways all of them are concerned with language in its relationship with society.

Communities

Individuals use language to:

- express themselves, exchange meaning, or influence others within language (or speech) communities
- demonstrate the independence of their political community, or
- symbolise their fellow-feeling and mutual dependence within an ethnic or national community.

So each of the disciplines is also concerned with a different type of community.

Speech communities and the standard language

People who use the same language – French, English, German – belong to a speech community. All speakers of German[1] do not necessarily share the same interpretation of specific words or even the same grammatical forms; the Austrian speech community could be distinguished from the Swiss, although both are subsets of the German speech community. The narrowest possible speech (sub-) community is probably an individual family, sharing the same jokes and the same understanding of what a particular word means for them: the widest is the total number of speakers of a language, including even those with the merest acquaintance with it – holidaymakers, or those who have learned the language at school in a foreign country.

It is the speech community that defines the standard language as such. A dialect becomes a standard through a historical sequence of stages: first being selected from among those available, then being codified and elaborated, and finally being accepted. These stages are not conscious, deliberate actions but happen by consensus and agreement. Furthermore, these processes are never finished for any living language: the social processes of selection and acceptance can mean that a new standard is being developed as social or political circumstances change. This has happened, for example, in the case of the German of Communist East Germany, which until the fall of the Berlin Wall in 1989 looked set to become a new standard but in fact simply disappeared. Nor are the linguistic processes of codification and elaboration finished. Language Academies in France and Spain continue to codify language, and there have been many attempts to modify spelling rules in other languages – including German, where an agreement between a number of countries in 1996 changed the traditional look of the language quite drastically.

Elaboration – the addition of new vocabulary to cope with changing circumstances or new technologies – is constant and necessary for all living languages, and in most has been very active in recent years with the invention and spread of computers and the information revolution. Codification is however the key stage for the standard language: it aims to ensure fixed values for the individual words and grammatical elements in a language system. This means that variation in meaning, in grammar, in spelling and pronunciation must be prevented by selecting fixed conventions to be implemented by all speakers as the only 'correct' ones. The whole notion of standardisation is thus bound up with the aim of the functional efficiency of the language: it must work, like the coinage or official weights and measures, as an effective and efficient guarantor of the value of individual words and phrases. Necessary change involving new words, and the expressions and grammatical forms which correspond to new ideas, also have to be in some way systematised and codified. As a result, there is constant creative tension in a living language between these two forces.

Once the standard language has been selected, codified, and elaborated, it must fulfil at least five functions to enable the speech community to accept it (Garvin 1993). It must:

1. unify the speech community and strengthen solidarity
2. form a boundary between this speech community and others and thus exclude members of other speech communities
3. confer prestige on the community and on the individual who masters it
4. act as a frame of reference for ideas of linguistic correctness
5. help its community, through the stage of elaboration and evolution, both to partici-pate in a full range of subject areas or domains – such as science, culture and

technology – and also keep up with and develop modern and changing thought and practice.

Once accepted, the standard language is the basis for its speech community's language attitudes. Speakers are loyal to it, have pride in it, are aware of – and defend – its norms of usage: through it, their desire to participate both in the full range of activities of human life and also in modern developments is realised. These language attitudes are often contradictory: purism – the defence of norms and the attitude that ensures codification is effective – attempts to keep the language static, while the desire to take part in the world means that the community must agree to accept dynamic change in the language. Such contradictions often provoke language problems, many of which come about because the speech community tries to take on the role of the political community or vice versa. So politicians may feel it is their duty to try to impose norms of speech on the community, or to impose one set of words rather than another – *native* words rather than *borrowed* ones. Although every linguist agrees that such language policy is generally doomed to failure (it is the usage of the speech community that eventually confirms what is right and wrong, not the laws of the political community) many political representatives keep trying.

The political community and the official language

A political community comes together to govern itself collectively, at the highest level, as an independent State. As part of this process, it decrees that it will use one language – or very rarely more than one language – as its official means of communication. The State may try to prevent other languages spoken within its borders – in peripheral regions, or by large groups of immigrants – from having the status of being official: it may determine the precise domains (Parliament, the law, education, even commerce or entertainment) in which the official language should be used. The State decides whether to pass laws consecrating an official status in such domains, as has happened in France, for example, or whether to accept a *de facto* situation and a working language as having official status, as is the norm in Britain (cf. Ager 1996c). An official language necessarily has high status, and the attitudes of members of the political community towards their language will be similar to those of the speech community, although with added vigour since it is very likely that the political majority may have to contend with one or more minorities. In particular, it is here that the concept of language as being intimately associated with identity may be pushed to extreme lengths in policy actions designed to ensure the supremacy of the (majority within the) political community itself.

Ethnic communities and minority languages

The third type of language community is that formed by an ethnic group, sharing (what they regard as) common origins, traditions, customs and usually language. Such ethno-linguistic communities are also speech communities, and as such may use a common standard language for their own purposes. They may be majority or minority political communities within the State But if they form a minority community, they must be prepared at some stage, usually in later life, to learn the language of the host political community. Ethnic communities may be (subordinate) political communities, depending on how much control over their own affairs they are granted by the superordinate State in which they live.

Linguistic or ethno-linguistic minorities are traditionally said to belong to one of two categories: those which are indigenous to the country and have an established regional and territorial base, such as the Welsh, and those which have no territorial base, such as Jews or immigrants. Both territorial and non-territorial minorities may be minorities in one political community and at the same time majorities in another. Dutch and German speakers in Flanders and Alsace are in a minority in France but clearly in a majority in the political communities of Holland and Germany respectively. In these cases it can happen that the standard language of the minority in one country is not the same as the standard elsewhere, and this is a common feature of migrant communities.

Two well-established minority communities present in most European countries are the Jews and the Gypsies, and the linguistic situation they represent is even more complex. For the Jewish community the standard language should logically be Hebrew, although apart from its liturgical use Hebrew has often dropped from normal use outside Israel. Romany has never been standardised and, although the many varieties spoken in different regions and different countries retain overall similarities, they reflect the chequered history of interaction between host and nomadic communities.

The minority community's behaviour and its language attitudes are necessarily conditioned by what may be seen as domination by the needs of the majority – which itself is probably also an ethnic community – or by accommodation to these needs on the part of the minority community. Three types of consequential behaviour on the part both of the majority and of the minority are possible: conflict, co-operation or compromise, and the nature and extent of these may characterise language policy as practised by the political authorities within the relevant political community. What is more, this language policy may apply to much more than language: much social welfare policy, regional economic policy and policy in a range of domains may be dictated by majority-minority relations within the political community, so it is hardly surprising that decentralisation is often symbolised by support for regional languages, while centralisation weakens their position.

These social and political facts about minority communities may lead to another quirk: in some political communities, it may happen that the prestigious language is that of a numerical minority, whereas it is the language of the majority that is in fact despised and treated as though it were the downtrodden language of a minority. This situation, characteristic of what happens in former colonies such as Niger or even South Africa, can happen even in countries like Britain where the dialect/accent of a social minority – Received Pronunciation – enjoys considerable status over the dialects/accents of more numerous social groups. In the case both of regional languages, and also of social dialects, 'minority' languages and communities seem to accept an inferior role, and such a community ends up despising itself and its language. On the other hand, many situations have arisen in the past when such a downtrodden group revolts and reverses the status and importance of its language. Something like this has happened in Belgium in the period since the Second World War as the numerically preponderant Flemish have realised their power, while the growth of regional autonomy in Spain reflects rejection of 'Madrid power'. In Peter the Great's time, Russian was regarded as the language of the peasantry and the Court spoke French, as indeed it did in eighteenth-century Prussia, and it took a considerable time before the language of the peasant majority obtained greater prestige. Self-despising speakers of regional dialects are to be found in most European societies, sometimes considering their own language as not really 'proper' English, French, or German, and demonstrating a degree of insecurity about their own linguistic forms which reflects the lack of social prestige they enjoy.

Links between communities and language

Speech, political communities and ethnic communities may be quite different from each other in their composition, in the ways in which their members are linked together, and in the role that language may play for them. The vast numbers of English speakers scattered throughout the world who belong to the English-speech community have no connection at all with the British State, and even less with England. In another case, the French and Flemish (Dutch) speakers in Belgium obviously belong to different speech communities. They form different 'ethnic' communities inspired by different traditions, emotions and sense of belonging, and yet form one political community – at least in some aspects of political life. The ethnic community may not be at one with either the speech or the political community.

Language can bind each of these types of community together, but the language which each accepts as a link between its members – but also as a barrier to other such communities – may play a different part and have a different status in each case. Thus the speech community bases the link on accepting a standard language; the political community takes what is usually also a standard language but calls it an official language and uses it for purposes of government and administration. The ethnic community, particularly if it is a political minority within the State, often uses its minority language as a symbol of its existence. Language – except in the case of the speech community – is not an essential element of the definition of what it means to be a community, and indeed there are many examples of ethnic communities which have completely lost their original language but have nonetheless retained a strong sense of nationalism, and, on the other hand, of multilingual political communities.

Three types of link connect language and community: the geolinguistic, the functional and the chronological (Truchot 1994). The link may be 'geolinguistic', in the sense that there is a close relationship between the language and a geographical region. In this case people may be monolingual and feel no need for any other language: their communication needs, their political needs and their emotive needs are served by one language in one territory. However, throughout the world, monolingual political communities are comparatively rare, and the society may have to solve its needs by using more than one language for different functions: one for administrative purposes, another for commercial needs, and yet another for education. Belgium is in this position: in functional terms the country needs both Flemish and French, and the country is bilingual. Such societal bilingualism may be – but does not have to be – accompanied by individual bilingualism: individuals in Belgium are often bilingual but many of them are not, at least at first. The need may grow in later life, however, and a 'chronological' link between community and language may emerge: the individual, at first monolingual, comes to realise that economic or social progress will be improved by acquiring the second language. These three types of link (geolinguistic, functional and chronological), between three types of language (standard, official and ethnic/minority) and three types of community (speech, political and ethnic), may already seem to present an enormously complex picture.

There is one further aspect of language(s) which needs to be considered before we see how far the attitudes of individuals or groups towards the situation may simplify what actually happens in reality. Languages are rarely monolithic: their pronunciation, word selection or indeed grammar can vary greatly from one geographical area to another, from one social group to another and also from one function or purpose to another. In English, for example, the regional dialects of the North show major differences of pronunciation with those of the South (*book, bus*) and many words in common use in Halifax are quite unknown in Truro or used in quite different ways (in parts of Yorkshire, *ginnel* is used for 'alleyway', *while* in the sense of 'until').

People who move up in the social or economic world often find that they use two or more social dialects: one in the pub to friends, another to the managing director. Similarly, the functional differences between the language of religion (in Church services or prayers) and the law (in Court, or in a legal document) are quite striking, and teachers would feel uncomfortable in using language which is too slangy when trying to explain Pythagoras' theorem. In some societies different languages may be used for these different functions rather than different dialects of the same language. Some Churches still use Latin as the language of prayer; in Alsace, shop assistants use the Alsace dialect of German to some clients and the 'posher' French to others; English or American has become an international language for pop music.

In practice, the range of language possibilities – which language or language variety to use when, to whom, for what purpose – presents few difficulties for adults who have achieved a level of social competence. However, there are problems for many in obtaining this social competence: for ethnic minorities, for recent immigrants, for the upwardly mobile, for social or charity workers or Members of Parliament who come across the deprived for the first time in their lives and need to communicate with them in their language. The attitudes which individuals or communities may have or show towards language-use often reflect such difficulties, and in this sense language-use may come to symbolise a community. In addition, it can symbolise the way that community sees itself, the ways individuals see themselves as belonging to or refusing membership of a community, and a number of other aspects of social life. There has long been a belief that two Englishmen could very quickly establish their relative social standing through the exchange of brief pleasantries about the weather.

Plan of the book

We deal firstly with the viewpoint of linguistics. We give a brief survey of linguists' descriptions of some languages, and, for Europe's six main languages, of the process by which specific dialects came to be used as the standard.

The second and subsequent chapters are more sociological and political. The second looks at language shift, and asks what makes individuals wish to acquire a new language. There is no doubt that the reasons are mainly external to the languages themselves. Pressures to obey a political power, to conform to social requirements, to improve the economic and financial position of the group or family, have led to the examples of 'bottom-up' language planning that we examine.

The third chapter traces the political role adopted by some States in protecting, supporting or disseminating their own official language – 'top-down' language planning. European States have in many cases decreed that one language rather than another shall be their symbol and their instrument, and that they have special responsibilities in shaping and modifying it to conform to their requirements.

The fourth chapter looks at the way States behave towards the linguistic and ethnic minorities living within their territory.

Migration from outside the continent to countries within it – the subject of the fifth chapter – has increasingly disturbed the fantasy 'ideal' that Hitler and his party so simply described in the 1930s: one race, one nation, one language, one people.

In the final chapter, we survey the likelihood that the dream of voluntary multilingualism might be achieved. Could there be an agreed language policy for Europe? Could using an artificial language help reduce the inevitable conflicts? How far can the language industries and the information society help to ensure that Europe becomes a supportive community rather than the background to dissension and the field of battle? What is the future for Europe's languages?

The purpose of the book is to bring together an approach to European languages which is not purely linguistic nor purely political, but assesses how far languages and the political, social and economic context in which they are used must necessarily interact. Languages are the fundamental means by which human beings communicate with each other, and the problems society poses cannot be solved in terms solely of the traditional social sciences – politics, sociology and economics – divorced from the idea of communication, nor in terms of a study of languages divorced from the settings in which they are used.

What do we mean by Europe? The geographical area is usually broadly defined as ranging from the Atlantic to the Urals, and from Novaya Zemla and the North of Scandinavia to the Bosporus and the southern edges of the Mediterranean, Black Sea and Caspian Sea. Turkey is generally excluded; Azerbaijan, Armenia and Georgia are sometimes included and sometimes not; Greece is included. Israel is often regarded as part of Europe – it is, after all, a participant in the Eurovision song contests – while Jordan, Iraq and Iran are not. Historically, European civilisation, as commonly understood, is that of the Greeks and the Romans. But Judaism, Christianity and Islam have each marked and affected it and continue to do so. Intellectually and culturally, European ideas have dominated the world, to the extent that it is still difficult for Chinese philosophies of science or Indian painting and music to make their voices heard.

From a linguistic approach, European languages in their diversity, in their specific political roles and in their social and economic functions, are an important part of the wealth of humanity. This book is intended to examine the basis for celebrating that wealth and that diversity.

Notes

1. cf Clyne 1996, who describes the 'pluricentric' German speech community. German is official in five countries (Germany, Austria, Switzerland, Luxembourg, Liechtenstein) and is used in Belgium, Italy, France, Hungary, Romania and Russia, as well as in many non-European countries.

Linguistic approaches to European languages

There are two main methods of classifying languages:

1) the genetic, relying on the history of the development of languages from a common ancestor, and
2) the typological, comparing linguistic systems across languages.

By studying their history, it is possible to group the world's languages quite systematically. Languages – with their component dialects – thus fall into groups or 'families'. These families themselves are regrouped into 'stocks', which fall into less than twenty main groups in the world, called 'phyla'.

European languages are classed into one of four phyla: Indo-Hittite, Caucasian, Uralic and Altaic. However, it should be remembered that speakers of languages from many other phyla have migrated towards Europe over the centuries and particularly in recent times. There is one European isolate – Basque – which does not seem to have much resemblance with any other known human language (Ruhlen 1987).

The Indo-Hittite phylum can be subdivided into two stocks – Indo-European and Anatolian – although the only language in this latter stock (Hittite) is now extinct. Although there can be no certainty, it is likely that proto-Indo-Hittite was spoken by dwellers in the steppes of southern Russia about 4,000 BC, and spread West from here towards the Danube area of Europe and beyond between 500 and 1,000 years later. At a similar time, movements East and South towards northern India and Iran were happening, where the Indo-Aryan or Indo-Iranian family of languages developed.

Indo-European languages are now numerous, falling into eight families and a number of sub-groups.

- Armenian,
- Indo-Iranian. (Includes, for example, Hindi and, in a separate classification, Farsi and Kurdish),
- Albanian
- Greek
- Italic (Comprises two groups, one containing the Romance languages – Italian, Spanish, French)
- Celtic
- Germanic (English and German together with Dutch, Yiddish and Swedish fall here), and

- Balto-Slavic (Languages like Lithuanian are placed in a different group from the Slav languages like Russian, Polish or Bulgarian).

Caucasian languages include Georgian, and in another group, Chechen. The area between the Black and Caspian Seas has a high concentration of languages, each spoken by a comparatively small number of people. Chechen, for example, is said to have less than a million speakers.

Uralic languages include, in one of the two stocks, Hungarian, Finnish and Estonian. Proto-Uralic is thought to have been spoken in the region of the northern Ural mountains about 7,000 or more years ago. Today the main language of the group is Hungarian, spoken by some 15 million speakers in Central Europe, isolated from other members of the group, while Finnish has only some 5 or 6 million speakers.

Altaic languages, on the border of Europe, include Turkish, Azerbaijani, Uzbek and Kazakh. Farther East, Mongolian and, a longer way from Europe, Japanese and Korean. There is little evidence of an early written form for these, and the earliest archaeological remains for Turkic, for example, date from the eighth century.

Basque, spoken in northern Spain and part of France, is a language isolate with no known connections with other languages in the world.

The typological method of classification of languages differs from the genetic in that it examines the structures of languages at the same point in time – i.e. now – and establishes similarities and differences between languages from this evidence alone. However, there is no one agreed basis for typological comparison.

Comparison could be based on:

- Vocabulary. In French, for example (by contrast with German), new words are formed by semantic change, borrowing (particularly from English) or by a limited use of prefixes and suffixes. In German, compounding is much more frequent.
- Similarity between sound systems or between pronunciation characteristics: the presence or absence of nasal vowels or of fricatives such as the 'ch' in the Scottish *loch*.
- Similarites or differences between grammatical systems.

In grammar, particularly in morphology, languages seem to fall into three types, according to how relationships are shown.

1. In isolating (analytic or root) languages – to a certain extent, English is like this – words are invariable and grammar is based on the order of the words.
2. In inflecting (synthetic or fusional) languages like German, endings are typically added to words to show grammatical relationships, and
3. In agglutinative (agglutinating) languages like Turkish or Finnish, words are built up from sequences of units, each of which expresses a particular grammatical function.

Yet other grammatical or stylistic characteristics are word order or the order of functional elements such as subject or object, as the language is spoken or written. In some languages words are used in a fairly strict order, so pronouns used before a verb – in French, for example – must follow a set sequence: *il le lui y a donné*, as opposed to the freer possibilities in English, such as *he gave it (to) him there, he gave him it there*, and *it was there that he gave it him* (although *'he gave it there him'* is impossible). Similarly, the order of the four elements subject (S), verb (or verb phrase) (V), object (O) and complement (C), is often used as a method of classifying languages into types such as VSO or SVO languages. Comparison between languages could be based on differences in the order of appearance of new information (the theme), as opposed to known information (the rheme) in 'functional sentence perspective'.

Comparison can also be based on the actual use of language elements:

* the relative frequency of a particular sound, type of word or grammatical element in a corpus of written or spoken text
* the nature of the linguistic context in which such items appear.

Overall, typological approaches reveal interesting insights about language and about linguistic processes but have proved not to have the lasting value in identifying language groups that the genetic method has.

Some European languages: development and description of standard languages

The following review briefly outlines linguistic characteristics of some languages, and in the case of the six most widely used ones, traces the history of the development of the standard language through four stages: selection of the most appropriate dialect, codification, elaboration, and eventual acceptance.

The West
Celtic languages and Welsh[1]

Celtic languages fall into three groups: the Goidelic /Gaelic (Irish, Scottish Gaelic, Manx); the Brythonic/British (Welsh, Cornish and Breton); and the Continental (now extinct). All surviving and attested languages seem to share a number of linguistic features, including initial mutation, where the first phoneme of a word varies according to a 'trigger' which is often grammatical (e.g. in feminine singular nouns after the article, or in possessive pronouns) but may also be phonological (involving prefixing consonants like 'n' or 'h' before words beginning with a vowel). Celtic languages have two genders, the prepositions are inflected, and there is an impersonal verb form. Word order is basically VSO; verbs are accompanied by preverbal particles which indicate features such as a negative, interrogative or subordination. Four features seem thus to characterise Celtic languages generally: mutation, word order, particles and inflected prepositions.

In Welsh, the change in an initial consonant can be 'soft', nasal or aspirate. So *pont* (bridge) becomes *dan bont* (under the bridge), *fy mhont* (my bridge) or *ei phont* (her bridge). Grammatical triggers produce, for example, *un ferch* (one daughter), which comes from *merch* (daughter), while feminine singular nouns produce mutation in (an uninterrupted sequence of) the following adjectives: *merch dal, brydferth* (*tal* [tall], *prydferth* [pretty]). The change is widespread.

In soft mutation, p, t, c, b, d, g, m, ll, rh become b, d, g, f, dd, zero, f, l and r respectively, and the grammatical triggers include prepositions, inflected verbs, and inversion.

Nasal mutation (p, t, b, d and g to mh, nh, ngh, m, n, and ng respectively) only operates after *yn* (in) – *yn mhlas* (*plas* [place]).

Aspirate mutation (p, t, c and any vowel to ph, th, ch and h-plus-vowel) occurs for example after genitive pronouns (*ei hewythr* [to her uncle], *ewythr* [uncle]).

Word order is VSO, so 'the boy saw the man' is *gwelodd y bachgen y dyn*. The addition of the positive declaratory particle *fe* gives *fe welodd y bachgen y dyn*, and the negative particle *ni* produces *ni welodd y bachgen ddyn* (the boy did not see a man) – each particle giving consequential mutation of *gwelodd* and *dyn*. Quite apart from these sound changes, Welsh is subject to enormous pressures from English, particularly in the colloquial register and in the vocabulary. Literary Welsh and colloquial Welsh are thus often divided, and since many speakers read or write little in the language, the tendency is for yet greater borrowing. This is despite widespread education in Welsh, much terminological language planning, and considerable financial investment in the language and its survival.

Romance languages
French
The phonology and pronunciation of French give the language some special features among the Romance languages.

- Nearly all vowels are stressed; there are four nasal vowels, although these are denasalised in certain positions and one of them is in the process of disappearing.
- Many final consonants – often retained in spelling – are pronounced only in a phenomenon of word linkage, called 'liaison', where the consonant reappears before a vowel (e.g. *un bon ami*).
- Some palatal fricative consonants are quite frequent (e.g. *chat, juge, oignon*).

The effect of phrasal structures on pronunciation can also be heard in the appearance or disappearance of the unstressed 'e', whose use avoids having to pronounce 'difficult' consonantal groups like *Arc de Triomphe*.

Verbal inflection is not very complex, and nearly all new verbs enter in one class ending in '-er' in the infinitive (e.g. *sélectionner*). There seems to be a certain amount of change going on in the way verb tenses are now formed, with the simple past (*il parla*) disappearing from spoken French to be replaced by the use of an auxiliary verb (*il a parlé*), a process also affecting the future tense (*il parlera, il va parler*).

Noun phrases show concord – for example in indicating the plural – among components such as nouns, adjectives, articles and determiners.

This grammatical requirement is retained mainly in the written form and the spoken form has fewer indications of it – and this concord seems unstable in the contemporary speech of the young. *Les jeunes enfants aiment les vieux livres* thus shows seven markers of the plurals in the written form, but only three in the spoken. The singular-plural distinction is only rarely a factor in the choice of the alternatives *tu* and *vous*, which are more determined, as indeed in many Romance languages, by the solidarity / formality distinction than by the singular / plural one. The basic vocabulary of French derives from Latin, but much neologism comes about through borrowing – at the present moment particularly from English.

The development of the standard language has been well described (see Lodge, R. A. 1993). The break-up of the Roman Empire in about 450 AD, invasions by German-speaking Franks and others, and the growth of feudal structures throughout Gaul, caused a number of dialects of Gallo-Roman to develop. At least three of these had as much social, cultural and economic potential for use as the standard as the Francien dialect of the Paris region did.

In the northern *Langue d'Oïl* area, Norman was the language of the English court which laid claim to much of France while Picard was the language of the wealthy agricultural area just North of Paris. In the South, more than one of the dialects of the *Langue d'Oc* could boast cultural potential, and one of them, Lemosin, was approaching the point of becoming a preferred choice both for literature and for administration. Francien eventually triumphed, probably because it was the language of power.

The French kings increased their control over regions and areas, not only through military conquest but also through marriages of convenience, pacts and treaties, and indeed the crusade against the Albigensian heresy in southern France in 1230. However, local dialects and languages were used until well into this century. There were other factors besides the political: the gradual growth of printing, the concentration of the population around Paris or the cultural pre-eminence of Paris with its University. However, deliberate Edicts by the political authority (Edict of Villers-Cotterêts in 1539) are said to be the first example of French legislation on language.

Codification of the language was the task of the French Academy, founded in 1634, as soon as Richelieu, acting on behalf of the King, realised the advantages to the government such linguistic control could bring. State-managed codification was carried out by many different hands although the most visible forms were those affecting literary and courtly language. The work has continued and frequent declarations of public concern with dictionaries and grammars being published, although not solely by the Academy. In fact, the modern standard dictionary for literary language is the *Littré*, first published in 1863-72, and the grammar is that of the Belgian *Grevisse* (1932). Professional newspaper columnists frequently write columns on good usage, and the systematic, thorough and complete codification of modern standard French is far more the result of deliberate conscious intervention than that of either British or American English.

This extensive codification eliminated from literary language much of the vocabulary of rural, vulgar or technical matters. French became a disciplined, even stark, language, eschewing the creativity which had characterised earlier periods in its history. It imposed two beliefs which have much affected language attitudes in France since: a golden age of perfection requires little change, and any new word must be carefully examined for its *bienséance* or appropriateness before acceptance. The needs of technical, military and diplomatic growth however meant that the vocabulary had to continue adding new terms. Since it could not do so through adapting existing rural or technical terms, often it had to borrow words and expressions from Italian, Spanish, Arabic and other languages, and now does so, mainly, from English. If it does not borrow, French finds it very difficult to create new lexical items (Noreiko, S. 1993). Speakers borrow, but do so with a sort of guilty feeling, although terms from world-wide 'Francophonie' – for example, from Quebec or African speakers – are now slowly finding their way into dictionaries published in France for general use. It can be argued that this is officailly accepted now in order to prevent the greater evil of borrowing from American English.

It is only within the last century that the standard language has become so widespread in France, and so generally accepted. Nineteenth-century educational investment has succeeded in contributing to the creation of both a homogeneous State and a homogeneous language. This investment was reinforced by the constant and coherent government policy since the Revolution of 1789 – of integration into the nation-State through an effective, centralised and prestigious administration. Outside France, in 'Francophonie', the Parisian norm is widely accepted too, mainly because France itself forms about fifty per cent of world speakers of French and because in many countries only ten per cent or less of speakers use French. There are other reasons, among which is the prestige and centralisation of the French school system and its widespread imposition on the Empire.

Spanish

In pronunciation, Castilian – by contrast with Latin American Spanish – is notable for its interdental 'th' sound in a word like *cerveza* (beer) or *cima* (summit), where its use contrasts with the 's' of *sima* (abyss). By contrast with most other Romance languages, Spanish has no 'v' or 'z' sound, although the fricative 'x' is much used. Another contrast lies in the fairly widespread vowel alternation in some verbs and other words, involving diphthongisation: *podemos* and *puedo*. Verb tenses are formed with auxiliary verbs, to an extent greater than in most Romance languages. Another difference lies in the existence of two verbs 'to be' – *ser* and *estar* – with uses many learners of Spanish initially find difficult to distinguish. The standard order of elements is VO, and a subject pronoun is not always required.

Late Latin could be said to have developed into Spanish by about the tenth century (Entwistle 1962; Green 1987). Local dialects abounded, and the eventual choice of Castilian came about partly as a result of the military strength of those who succeeded, from the retaking of Toledo in 1085 to the (re)conquest of Grenada in 1492, in forcing the Arab invaders out of the peninsula. Castilian, as it spread South carried by wars and trade, separated the dialects of Léon and Aragon and established its literary supremacy in the thirteenth century. However, even in the twentieth century the conflict between regional languages has been severe, with Galician and Catalan banned under the Franco regime after 1939. The resultant fierce regionalism mixed with political opposition was one of the main factors which influenced the 1978 Constitution, which accords language rights to regional users. The strength of regional feeling is tragically exemplified by the continued existence and military activities of the Basque separatist organisation ETA. In the 1990s, nonetheless, the regions of Spain are so autonomous that they conduct their own political affairs in their local languages.

The codification of Castilian dates back to the sixteenth century, while the Royal Language Academy, founded in 1713, and producing its first dictionary in 1730, acts with caution in its fairly frequent, although minor, adjustments. A second Latin-American Spanish norm is based on the usage of Bogotá or increasingly of Mexico City. Language Academies were established throughout many Latin American countries in the nineteenth century, and there are now so many that there exists an association of Hispanic Academies. Elaboration, despite the influence of borrowings from American English (which are currently at a high level), takes place mainly by linguistic process such as suffixation or compounding (*parachoques* [bumper bar]). Borrowing has nonetheless marked Spanish at different times: from Arabic in medieval times, French during the eighteenth century, English now, but also from Latin American languages from where many words have indeed entered other languages: *canoa, piragua, cacique, hurucan*.

Because of the importance of regional differences in peninsular Spain, and the close association of politics and language, the Castilian form of Spanish, although widely accepted as the standard, has not been fully accepted, as such by all communities (Clyne 1992). Similarly, the number of political communities using Spanish across the world, the large and growing populations of Spanish speakers in South and increasingly in North America, mean that the future might bring yet further linguistic separation. Spanish is and remains a pluricentric language.

Portuguese
As with Spanish, the Latin American form of the language (Brazilian Portuguese) is widespread, and contrasts in major ways with the European. The Iberian Portuguese vowel system is more complex than that of most Romance languages, containing a number of diphthongs and also a range of nasal vowels and

diphthongs while stressed vowels also contrast with a range of unstressed ones. Stress generally, but by no means always, occurs on the penultimate syllable. In morphology, one of the striking features of Portuguese is the range of address forms, which includes not only the formal/informal contrast between singular and plural, i.e. *tu/vos*, but also the use of *você*, a range of phrases like *o senhor* and titles together with use of the third person as if it were a second person form. SVO is the standard sequence of elements, although as with French and Romanian, grammatical objects can be detached from the normal word order and thus be emphasised in a process called topicalisation.

Italian

The vowel system is fairly simple and tends to reduce to the standard five, while the consonants lack a clear 'z'. Nearly all words end in a vowel, except loan-words and one or two others. Interestingly therefore, and in contrast to French, plurals in Italian are usually marked by a change of final vowel – *casa/case*, *monte/monti* – and adjectives and articles change similarly. Verb tense forms are usually formed by the addition of suffixes and Italian verbs are usually regular. As in other Romance languages, there is a formality and politeness contrast in address, but here this is between the second-person singular *tu* and *Lei*, the third-person singular. Many words carry suffixes expressing the speaker's attitude: *ragazzino*, *ragazzetto*, *ragazzuccio*, *ragazzone*, *ragazzaccio*, *ragazzotto* give different opinions on *ragazzo* (boy), and some words bearing such suffixes have developed different meanings entirely from the original. Italian generally is a theme-rheme language, where the topic (known information) precedes what is said about it (new information) and the SVO element order is the norm.

As the Roman Empire collapsed, major dialectal divisions occurred creating Western and Eastern Romance. This dialect division separates northern Italian forms, which are closer to French, from southern ones, which are closer to Romanian (Migliorini and Griffith 1984). Many dialects developed within these divisions: although by the thirteenth century many Italian centres could claim some literary eminence, by the fourteenth the prestige of Florentine writers ensured preference for the Tuscan dialect. Nonetheless, the lack of political unity until 1861 meant that the question was not solved until a commission recommended Florentine for the new national school system.

The role of the *Accademia della Crusca*, the first European language Academy, was central to the task of codification. It based most of its work on literary texts, and Dante, Petrarch and Boccaccio were the models. Literary Italian is fairly conservative in its linguistic development; educated readers of today have little difficulty in understanding late medieval texts. Codification of the language did not present the same type of problem as in French or English. The general pressures in favour of Florentine included the special role of the Vatican through its political power and its attractiveness for Florentine speakers. 'Elaboration' in Italian has been much influenced by the comparative nearness of Italian and Latin.

The centuries during which Latin was raided as a source for technical, scientific and social concepts enabled much 'new' Italian vocabulary to be absorbed from ancient models.

Standard Italian has borrowed much from other dialects of the language, and continues to do so. Specialists have commented that the standard language lacks many common terms for which local variants are in common use. Hence it is not always clear in Milan that the words for 'stamp', 'meal', 'petrol', or 'draught beer' will be the same as those used in Naples or Sicily. French has acted through the centuries as the source of many words and continues to do so, as with English and German. In more recent times, Italian has been as much subject to American influence as most other languages. Some suffixes and prefixes are much used today to expand the vocabulary. Further, many of these words and processes have found a similar role in other European languages: super- (*supermercato*), mini- (*minigolf*), maxi- (*maximoto*), inter- (*interplanetario*); -izzare (*attivizzare*).

Despite the Manzoni Commission of the late 1800s, it is still to an extent doubtful that standard Italian has been accepted by the speech community as the language to be used, even in the most prestigious domains. It was only in 1982 that more than 50% of poll respondents showed that they regarded Italian (rather than a dialect) as their first language. In 1990, 57% preferred their dialect and some 15% did not know Italian at all; it may well be that a 'sub-standard' variety of popular Italian is as widespread a general means of communication as the formal norm. It is hardly surprising that linguistic rights are formally recognised in the Constitution for speakers of some other languages.

Romanian
Farther to the East, Romanian survived as a Romance language after the disappearance of the Roman Empire despite being surrounded by non-Romance languages, such as Hungarian, which have greatly influenced it. Consonant clusters like *skl*, *zv* and *zb*, and even *hl*, *ml* and *kt* (the latter three occurring at the beginning of words) are most unlike those in the remainder of Romance languages. Stress is a feature of the phonological and pronunciation systems. Like Italian, plurals are formed by vowel change rather than the addition of '-s'. In the morphology of the language, a three-case system has been retained for nouns and adjectives (nominative, accusative and dative) and another difference with most Romance languages is the suffixation of the definite article, giving *omul* (the man). This suffix can also transfer to associated adjectives, as with *omul bun* and *bunul om* (the good man). A vocative case exists also for animate beings, especially humans, and for proper names.

The normal order of elements is SVO, although OVS is a frequent alternative, probably due to the influence of Balkan languages, such as Greek. Verbs normally use an auxiliary to form the future and other tenses. In vocabulary, the Slavonic borrowings have been calculated as being as high as 40%, although most recent borrowings have been from other Romance languages – particularly French – and from international languages such as English.

The East
Slavonic languages
Russian

The Slav languages generally are closer to each other than the Romance languages are to each other. Most use the Cyrillic alphabet, although Czech and Polish do not, and use of the alphabet correlates with the Orthodox religion. Frequent sibilants seem to be a characteristic of Russian pronunciation, and originate in one of the two major differences between the Slav languages and other Indo-European languages – palatalisation and vowel gradation. The consonant system is in effect doubled through the presence of both a palatalised and a non-palatalised form for each consonant. In the vowels, stress is of major importance: it can occur on any syllable and can move from syllable to syllable in different forms of the word, with a major effect on weakening the distinctiveness of vowels like 'o' and 'a'. Vowel alternation, for example, between 'e' and 'o', or between the presence of a vowel such as 'o' (in *son*) and its absence (in the genitive *sna*), is another characteristic of Russian. Consonantal alternation, such as that between 'k' and 'sh' – both related to morphophonemic considerations – is also a feature of the language.

In morphology, the nouns and adjectives have six cases and plural inflections, while adjectives also indicate gender. Other morphophonemic features include the presence of singular, plural and dual number and the category of animate nouns that require alternative accusative forms. Verbal forms indicate person and number, and in the past forms, gender; indicating perfective and imperfective aspect is an important part of the system. Verbs also indicate a range of meanings through the addition of prefixes. In syntax, there is no article, and agreement of the phrase elements is required. Word order in the sentence is free in that grammatical sentences – with some change in meaning or stress on the elements – can occur with the elements in practically any order, following the general principle of a theme-rheme sequence.

Interestingly, Old Russian, first written about the year 1000 AD and a member of the East Slavonic dialect group, has developed into Russian, Byelorussian and Ukrainian – three modern languages, each with an accepted norm of its own (Comrie and Stone 1978; Comrie 1987). The first stage in selecting the norm seemed to choose Old Church Slavonic, a religious language from the South-Slavonic sphere, as a basis – a choice strengthened by 1453 as clerics fled to Russia. However, a specific proposal from Lomonossov in 1755, after Peter the Great's modernisation, proposed a mixture of South and East Slavonic dialect forms as the norm for the Russian Empire.

Codification took place comparatively late. The alphabet had been devised for Old Church Slavonic during medieval times by the monks Cyril and Methodius, and the modern Cyrillic alphabet is a direct descendant of their system. However, even by 1897, only 21 per cent of the population could read, only 13 per cent lived in towns, and the great mass of the population had to wait until after the Revolution to acquire any sort of education or understanding of the standard language. By 1970, over 99% of the population was said to be literate, and just over half lived in towns. Codification of the language used by the Bolsheviks was much resisted by the émigrés living outside Russia. However, this has resulted in a standard orthography, the adoption of a major spelling reform and many changes in vocabulary to reflect the social innovations, administrative methods and other changes introduced during Communism.

'Elaboration' of the vocabulary developed during Peter the Great's period, when a deliberate attempt was made to modernise the country. Changes were also taking place, although at a much slower rate, during the nineteenth century with the gradual development of industrialisation and technical innovations. The Revolution of 1917 obviously had a major influence on the vocabulary, and since 1989 there have again been great changes in the development of new words to cope with new realities. The acceptance of the norm as a compromise between East and South Slavonic means that the modern language retains features, even doublets in the vocabulary, from both main dialects. The Communist period too had considerable influence on ensuring the general acceptance of the norm; widespread education, the influence of the media, and the national feeling brought about by the Second World War did much to linguistically unite the population. Although standard Russian is now accepted in Russia, its sociolinguistic role elsewhere has been much reduced since 1989.

Polish
As with Russian, the consonant system is complex with palatalised forms contrasting with non-palatalised ones; a third possibility exists for some consonants where the place of articulation provides another variant. Double consonants are also frequently pronounced as such. Two nasal vowels are often heard, and others may be used before fricatives (*tramwaj, inspektor*). Polish words are generally stressed on the penultimate syllable. In morphology, seven grammatical cases are distinguished, and a grammatical distinction is made between animate and non-animate forms. There is a further contrast between most normal accusatives and masculine animate accusative in the singular and plural. Verbs show tense distinctions by inflections rather than the personal pronoun. The exception to this is where *pan* and the third person are used to express politeness, creating – in effect – an honorific second person. The aspect system is similar to that of Russian, as is that of the system of concord in word sequences and sentences.

The North
Germanic languages
German

German strikes many who hear it spoken as being basically a consonantal language, and twenty-one consonantal phonemes are normally distinguished. The front rounded vowels, spelt with an umlaut (*kühn*, *höre*), are said to give the impression of strength and vigour, although occasionally harsh. Compounding is a significant process in German for creating words, many of which are in English full noun phrases (e.g. *Rheindampfschiffsfahrtgesellchaft*). Nouns, adjectives, articles and pronouns are inflected for gender, number and case – and verbs indicate person, number and tense. This morphological system is very rich by comparison with most Germanic languages, and much of the meaning is conveyed by a governing category; for example, a preposition or a verb. Verb inflections indicate categories such as tense through suffixation or through vowel change. Word order, particularly the position of the verb, is a significant characteristic of German: the verb can be final, first or second in clauses – notably final in subordinate clauses.

Germany did not become one political community until Bismarck's unification process of the late 1800s. Prior to that time, there was no one political or cultural centre in the widespread German-speaking lands around which linguistic selection could formally take place. Low (northern), Central and Upper (southern) German were the three main dialects despite the existence of a southern compromise language and a northern commercial *lingua franca*, based on the economic power of the Hanseatic League (Keller 1978; Comrie 1987; König and van der Auwera 1994; Clyne 1996). But East Central German was eventually chosen: in law from 1400, in the dissemination of Luther's work through the printing press from 1450 and later in the military basis of Prussian power. Partly because of the pluricentric nature of German as it developed, codification of the language has taken a long time (cf. Clyne, M. (ed) 1992).

Other factors also delayed codification: for most of the seventeenth and eighteenth centuries German was marked as the language of Protestantism and of the lower orders (French was used in Royal and polite society, Latin for education). German was greatly affected by regional variation or by borrowing from other languages. Regional varieties, such as Bavarian and Swabian, were codified and standardised first: the Austrian version – the language of a large Empire until 1918 – is still regarded by Austrians as being of equal status to the North German standard. From the late eighteenth century Adelung's dictionary and spelling rules, published between 1774 and 1786, formed the basis for standard German; Konrad Duden's work was accepted in Prussian schools from 1880, and the authorities in Austria and Switzerland also applied them. Theodor Siebs 'Theatre speech' ('*Deutsche Bühnensprache*') of 1898 was in reality much more than a dictionary of pronunciation. Although German has no Academy, it does have a prestigious language planning organisation in the Mannheim Institut für Deutsche Sprache, which monitors linguistic changes and provides research and information on language matters for the relevant Government commissions. While the spelling reform proposed in 1954 was agreed by the Federal Republic and the GDR, the Swiss voted against and the Austrians were deadlocked, so at that point it was still not easy to be sure about international control of the language. In 1996 however the Culture and Education Ministries of Germany, Switzerland, and Austria agreed a reform covering more than just spelling; the German minorities in Italy, Liechtenstein, Romania, Belgium and Hungary were also involved in the final agreement.

The process of 'elaboration' is mainly carried out in German through the linguistic device of compounding, enabling it to construct nouns of breathtaking complexity and to cope easily with changes in word-meaning including in particular technical advances. Towards the end of the German Democratic Republic, for example, the Duden dictionary published in the East contained about 75,000 entries while that produced in the West had about 110,000: most of the Western developments were concerned with technical change and most were derived from compounding (Clyne 1996, 67-73). German also borrows terms from other languages with ease (e.g. *checken*, *Knowhow*).

High German has been formally accepted by the three main (Austria, Germany and Switzerland) and two lesser (Luxembourg, Liechtenstein) European political communities as their norm. Outside these countries there remain a number of ethnic minorities scattered throughout Europe and abroad: these also generally accept the standard as agreed, with perhaps one important exception. Yiddish, the form of German in use among Jews, is so widespread – particularly in the New World – that it could be said to offer an alternative language.

English

The English word stock consists of items derived from the original Germanic roots together with a substantial overlay of words – almost half – borrowed from French after the Norman conquest and since. Most grammar words are Germanic; many Latinate words represent educated or elitist interests and concerns. English, in fact, is characterised by its hospitality to borrowing, which it seems to prefer to the Germanic processes for enriching the vocabulary through compounding and adding prefixes or suffixes. Nonetheless, compounding, as in *bookshop*, prefixing, as in *hyperinflation*, and suffixation, as in *decimalisation*, are active processes.

In phonology and pronunciation, English is notable for its reduction of unstressed vowels to 'e' (e.g. *a* or *the*), for its eight diphthongs (*gate, dive, toy, home, house, dear, fair, door*) and the triphthongs (*fire, flower, fear, fewer*). Five long vowels and seven short ones including the unstressed vowel complete the range. In consonants, the two interdental 'th' sounds (e.g. *thin* and *then*) and the four sibilants (e.g. 'sh' in *shame*, 's' in *measure*, 'ch' in *chin* and 'j' in *judge*) mark differences with other Germanic languages; the final sound of a word like *drinking* is another frequent component in pronunciation. Some syllables in words are stressed or made more prominent by a combination of pronunciation factors such as stress, pitch, and length. Stress is often the only marker of a difference in meaning, as in a word like *object* (noun and verb): a many-syllabled word can have a number of main and secondary stresses (e.g. *proliferation*).

Spelling is quite often unrelated to pronunciation, and the traditional example is the variety of vowel sounds hidden by the one spelling 'ough' in *plough, rough, cough, ought, through, borough, dough*. Another example is George Bernard Shaw's spelling of *fish* as *ghoti* (*cou'gh', w'o'men, na'ti'on*).

English syntax is generally felt to be exceptionally versatile, enabling relations among elements to be expressed in a variety of ways. Word order is mainly SVO, and meaning is normally signalled through word order rather than through inflection. Phrasal verbs (verbs with a preposition: e.g. get–*about, ahead, along, at, away, back, by, down, in, off, on, out, over, round, through, up*) are a characteristic of the language, and auxiliary verbs are used to express tense, mood and voice (e.g. *he did write, do write, the letter was written*). Noun phrases are occasionally complex and almost infinitely extensible (e.g. *the University management team car bumper sticker's top end fell off*).

The dialect which was most likely to become the standard for England at a point in time just before the Norman Conquest of 1066, was West Saxon, which had by then achieved the status of a national preferred literary form and, as the language of Alfred the Great, had political as well as cultural importance (Baugh, A.C. and Cable, T. 1978; Burchfield, R. 1994). The Norman Conquest, however, was a major blow, and it very nearly succeeded in imposing Norman French on the conquered people as both the standard and official language. However, in 1204 King John's loss of Normandy, and the Black Death of 1348, had the linguistic effect of making English more widespread and prestigious. One proof of this is the Statute of Pleading of 1362, which required English rather than French or Latin to be used in the Courts. Gradually, over the period up to 1600, most writing reflected East Midlands usage, and a number of main influences converged to bring about the preponderance of this dialect. These influences were bureaucratic practice (the language of the King's clerks), literature (Chaucer), education and learning (Oxford and Cambridge), political power (the London Court) and the prestige of the printed form after Caxton's invention of the printing press in 1476. The selection was hence as much social as political.

After selection came codification, which took place from about the sixteenth century through the publication of dictionaries and grammars. Many of them intended to teach the language to squires in the country or to the Welsh after the Act of Union between England and Wales in 1536. The particularly significant texts were Jonathan Swift's 'Proposal for Correcting, Improving and Ascertaining the English Tongue' in 1712; the grammar of Bishop Lowth in 1762, and Samuel Johnson's Dictionary in 1755. At no point in this process was the State openly involved. The influences were administrative, legal and literary language, and the English of education and the Church. 'Received Pronunciation', accepted as the spoken standard, also developed through education, particularly that given in the nineteenth-century public schools. This was followed in the early twentieth century by cinema, radio and television which produced 'BBC English'. The codification of English has produced at least two standard languages in the British and North American forms.

The third stage is elaboration, or the systematic addition of new vocabulary and expressions. To do this, English borrowed extensively, particularly from French, Latin and Greek. English today is recognised as a language in which it easy to introduce new linguistic forms, and although borrowing has continued (*teriyaki, taco*), there are two main processes of neologism. First, semantic change (a *mouse* is useful in computing), and second lexical creativity through new word sequences (*battered baby syndrome*), new adjectives (*machine-readable*), prefixation (*dis-information*), suffixation (*institution-al-isation*) and the use of one word-class as another (*to leaflet; a gay; down-sizing*).

The English speech community 'accepts' the standard language by using it in specific public domains, particularly the Press, the law, government, and latterly in education, where its use has only been prescribed since the National Curriculum was adopted in 1994. England is not quite the same as Britain: in Wales, Welsh never quite dropped out of use even in the public domain. The British speech community still does not altogether accept the standard language, and certainly does not accept a standard pronunciation. This fact has been grasped more and more by political speakers in recent years, and the obligatory acceptance of the standard has become practically a shibboleth of recent British Ministers of Education, who seem fond of declaring the necessity of its adoption. Outside England, a standard English, although it is not quite the same as British English, is generally accepted. This often corresponds to the American standard rather than the British one since Britain's population and world influence form a minority among the world's English speakers.

The South
Altaic languages
Turkish
Although Turkish is not usually included as a European language, a brief description may show some of the differences characteristic of Altaic languages in general. The salient features most linguists distinguish about Turkish are vowel harmony, verb-final word order, agglutination, and nominalised subordinate clauses. Together, these make Turkish and many of the Turkic languages quite different from Indo-European languages. The eight vowels are normally short, but long vowels do occur – either 'naturally' or as a result of the disappearance of a velar fricative, which is no longer pronounced. The vowels within a word are determined by the first: if this is a back and/or a rounded vowel, the following ones (for example in the morphemes for plural or case) will also be back and/or rounded. The consonantal system includes palatalised fricatives, and, in general, consonant clusters are avoided initially and only allowed in restricted fashion

elsewhere. As with the vowels, consonants are affected by other consonants which precede them, and may add features like voice, devoicing, or even disappearance according to the construction of the syllable and word. Stress is in general word-final. Turkish morphology is based on agglutinative suffixes: that is, grammatical characteristics are indicated by the addition of morphemes to the stem. Suffixes indicating word class may be added first in a sequence – 'give', 'profit', 'profitable' and 'profitability', would be *ver*, *verim*, *verimli*, then *verimlilik*. Morphemes would be added to these, indicating number, agreement or case for nouns and adjectives, or giving voice, negation, mood and tense. The unmarked word order is SOV, although in Turkish it is fairly free. The subordinate or embedded clauses Indo-European languages use often take nominalised form in Turkish: the embedded 'verb' adopts noun-like suffixes.

The Centre
Uralic languages
Hungarian

Hungarian is not at all like the Indo-European languages in most of Europe. Hungarian is also, however, unlike most Uralic languages. There are seven vowels, with both long and short forms, and it is important to note that stem-vowels govern the vowels of suffixes. Hence, vowel harmony affects the nature of the word together with its suffix. In some cases, this requirement can lead to the dropping of the suffix verb altogether. Among consonants there is a group of palatalised and non-palatalised forms affecting the dentals, fricatives and the nasal 'n'. Consonants following each other are affected by assimilation. In conjugation, verbs consist of a stem followed by two suffixes – one indicating tense and mood, the other person and number. The form of these suffixes may vary according to a number of factors, some of which are to do with the surrounding morphemes and others with the nature and person of the object. These complications provide a number of different forms for apparently the same verb. Similarly, nouns consist of a stem followed by up to three inflectional suffixes – for number, person/possessor and case. The latter is divided into a fundamental locative distinction between stationary and moving (approaching or departing) and then into traditional categories, such as subject, object, possessor or instrument. Suffixes, added to nouns or verbs, may also indicate further types of meaning associated with the root form, and coverbs also affect the meaning or provide subtle additions to it. Hungarian vocabulary consists of numerous loan-words: from German, Romanian, Italian. Analysis of sentence perspective is basic to Hungarian word order: the central component of the theme occurs before the verb, while rheme is normally initial.

The linguist's view

The 'pure' linguist's view of the classification of European languages, fascinating though it is for the specialist, is limited. Both genetic and typological classification are based on language structure and language components, and on these alone. However, it soon becomes clear that languages are much more than this. Languages are not abstract entities; they are used by people in communities. Such communities are aware of other languages and civilisations nearby, borrowing from them according to need, often making a major change to the look and sound of the language. The languages themselves are affected by a range of factors, which in turn cause changes in, for example, the dominant dialect, the extent to which change is rapid or slow, the nature of change and even how regular or irregular individual forms can be. In addition, the context in which languages are used affects them in a number of ways:

- journalists delight in inventing new terms and in using language to shock
- creative literary artists do the same, and ensure new meanings and new thought are developed despite the restrictions of the language itself
- politicians use and abuse language in order to persuade voters to support them, and languages are put to use in the political world, and
- technical and social change gives new meanings to old words and forces people to invent new terms.

It is language, above all else, that enables groups of people to feel they belong to one community and to exclude others from membership. Further, it is by and through language that many people make their living, control others' economic destiny and ensure they play a part in the economic life of their community. We next consider how and why Europeans drop one language in order to adopt a new one.

Notes

1. Ball, M. J. (ed) 1993

Language, identity and the individual

There is little doubt that a particular language represents a specific physical and social reality. Although the English word 'bread' is translated as pain or brot the actual substance looks and tastes quite different in different countries. The same is true even of words for abstract concepts like truth and beauty, and the relationship between the words of one language and any 'universal' reality is usually different in both denotation and connotation from that in another: both the actual meaning of the word or phrase, and its implications and value, differ. Such cultural differences between societies are inevitable, but still generate considerable misunderstanding in international gatherings where politicians try to agree on what words like 'democracy' or 'federalism' mean. Similarly, discourse structures – the way an argument is presented, the way an audience is persuaded to accept a point of view, and even the format of a conversation or the opening of a telephone call – are quite differently understood in different speech communities.

From these evident truths, a whole philosophy of language and society has been constructed which postulates a close relationship between not merely the physical or mental constructs of the world outside, and the language in which they are expressed, but also between modes of thought and language, and says that one is determined by the other. The example given by two American linguists tried to show that time, as understood by the Hopi Indians, was quite different from time as understood in English: concepts of past, present and future were simply meaningless to the Hopi, for whom ancestors and unborn children were as present now as living people, and of equal importance, and time was expressed as a range of durations (Crystal 1987, 15, on the 'Sapir-Whorf hypothesis'). Applying this idea to French and English, one could say that for French, the meaning of 'justice' is determined by the fact that in France a judge, appointed by the State, (juge d'instruction) will determine the facts of a case against the background of formalised codes of laws, whereas for English in Britain, 'justice' will emerge through an adversarial fight between two lawyers in court, where the role of the State-appointed judge is merely to act as referee and to work within a history of previous legal decisions. Behind an apparently identical word there lie two wholly different philosophies, traditions, approaches and identities.

If language is a means of expressing and symbolising the society in which an individual lives, it is a short step to believing that the only form that society can take is that represented through its language, and, in the opposite sense, that a specific language can represent only one form of human society. The identity of a society, of the individuals within it, and of the way they think, is thus determined by their language; and consequently, every language and its set of meanings is unique. In this way, French, or Dutch, or Italian, could represent only that type of social organisation and set of values which has been constructed through French, Dutch or Italian, and the different societies could never be the same. Many problems are associated with this attitude and belief. To take one example, if the French language determines the values, traditions and culture of France and is thus a symbol of French identity, then French as used in countries which do not share that history or even those values must logically be a different language: Belgian French, Swiss French and Quebec French must decide either that they are different languages, or, if they all claim to be using French, their societies must accept the values, traditions and culture of France. Furthermore, changes to French language imply changes to French society, and social changes are impossible unless the language changes to permit them: without major changes in the way women are referred to in the language for example, the social position of women cannot be changed. The language must have the terms to express a thought before that thought can exist.

This is an extreme statement of the proposition that languages determine the way we think (linguistic determinism) and that the distinctions one language makes are not made by others (linguistic relativity). But the idea that language and society are closely linked; that language is a symbol of the identity of those making up society; and that a particular society is both unique and worth preserving, is widespread. It could be alleged for example that despite the fact that the same language (Serbo-Croat) was involved, the whole of the battle between Serbs and Croats in the former Yugoslavia turned on the different alphabets each uses (one Cyrillic, like Russian, and the other Roman), representing the different religions (Orthodox and Catholic), traditions, histories and beliefs each community cherishes. In the final analysis, war came about because one community wanted to impose its alphabet on the other(s)! Linguistic determinism and relativism lie behind the defensiveness of the French towards US influence; they are at the root of the ferocious independence of the Basques; they symbolise the break-down of Belgian harmony. Similarly, when it is said that languages are born, live in different degrees of health, and die, what is meant is that the relevant society – communities of individuals – decides to change from one language to another. Language shift is hence a phenomenon, not of languages, but of individuals and communities. It is people who adopt a new language, shift their allegiance from one language to another, allow a language to fall out of use. In some cases, the relevant community is forced to change loyalty and pushed into adopting a new identity. In other cases, the attractions of the new language outweigh the disadvantages, and the move is made voluntarily: the 'pull' factors outweigh the 'push' ones. The competition is however not a linguistic one: winning languages do not succeed because they are intrinsically better forms of communication, nor do losers disappear because they are not capable of expressing reality. The factors which bring about the change derive from the political, social or economic assessment made by the individuals using a language. In this chapter, we shall track the effect of these three types of pressure or attraction on the European language scene, looking in each case at what makes a group of people move away from a language as well as the attractions that entice them to adopt a new one. In effect, in this chapter we are studying language planning 'from the bottom up' – by people, acting together in a community.

Language shift: the political imperative

Individuals can be forced to change their language allegiance, or can adopt a new language because they wish to demonstrate their desire to be part of a political community. The use of French throughout France has responded to such a political imperative which if anything has grown stronger with the passage of time (Ager, D. E. 1996c). Before the French Revolution of 1789, the geographical area of what is now France (minus, at the time, the area around Nice and Savoy) used up to thirty different languages and dialects, including Basque, Breton, Catalan, Dutch, German, Italian and many different forms of the three main dialects which had developed from the Vulgar Latin spoken in the Roman Empire. The kings and aristocracy of the Ancien Régime were quite happy to leave local peoples to use whatever language they wanted, although they had to use a standard language, mainly French, in order to achieve social or economic advantage, for example at Court. Politically, there was no real pressure before 1789 for the common people to adopt the standard French of the Royal Court and the kingdom generally, or to abandon the use of their regional language or dialect. Although Royalty demanded loyalty, the country remained a mosaic of separate fiefdoms and 'particularisms', and political pressure, if there was any, was to show support for these by retaining local languages. Politically, the governing power, the king, in whom sovereignty resided, was just not interested in how subjects communicated with each other, but in the communication of the Royal will to the subjects of the realm. For the aristocracy, of course, the situation was different, and there are many references to the 'gasconisms' new courtiers had to lose quickly if they wished to gain political favour from the Royal Court.

The Revolution changed the situation dramatically, in that the process of government – to a certain extent – moved from 'top-down' to 'bottom-up'. Sovereignty lay in the people, and for them to participate they needed to be able to communicate, not merely with the rulers but also between themselves. Ordinary people had the right to the language of enlightenment and progress and to the means of expression which would give them access to thought, science and culture, and were desperate to acquire it. Associated with this change from the duties of the subject to the rights of citizens was another struggle. To a certain extent, this contradicted the 'pull' notion of the attraction of equality, leading to much greater centralisation – and concentration – of power, as well as the imposition of French on those who did not possess it. The first examples of this were the 'linguistic terror' in Alsace where those using German dialect, even in promulgating the ideas of the Republic, were regarded as traitors. The political imperative was outlined in the Abbé Grégoire's report of 1794 on the 'necessity and means for destroying dialects and generalising the use of French', and also in Barère's speeches in Parliament when he condemned 'federalism and superstition' in those speaking Breton; 'emigration and hatred of the Republic' in speakers of German; 'the counterrevolution' in those using Italian and 'fanaticism' in speakers of Basque. 'Among a free people language must be one and the same for all' (Lodge 1993, 214).

The political motivation for educational progress, and for language as the cornerstone of this, has been the basis for much of French policy, including the development of the uniquely French approach to colonisation and the colonies. The policy has been followed consistently: regional (and immigrant) languages have no formal status even today, and French has been consecrated as the Republic's official language in the Constitution and through legislation such as the Toubon Law of 1994. Language-based nationalism and its political manifestations are not aimed solely at making declarations, however; they symbolise a battle in which there is an enemy to destroy. This enemy has usually been the minority language or languages within the border of the political State, although the 'enemy' may also be the language of another State or States. The political intention is to kill off these languages, and what they symbolise: citizens are either forbidden to use them, or to use them in subordinate functions only. However, these political intentions are not the 'top-down' autocratic instructions of leaders remote from the feelings and desires of the population: they represent a 'pull' factor, as opinion polls in France supporting these actions have shown. An example of this happened most recently in 1994, when government's attempts to discourage the use of English were generally welcomed.

The importance of language loyalty to the creation of the State, and hence the centrality of the political factor in it, is shown in recent Spanish history too (Green, J. 1987). Franco's control of the Spanish state, as a consequence of his Party's victory in the Civil War in 1939, led to thirty-five years of rule during which the identity of the regions and their languages, were consistently minimised. Their languages had no official role and, from the point of view of the central government, Madrid was right to keep their status low: much of the opposition to Franco and his politics was based on or associated with language opposition. The Basque independence movement claimed the use of the Basque language as a symbol of its political demands. Catalonia, one of the strongest anti-Franco regions, used Catalan as the marker of the political stance of much of its population. After Franco's death, the battle within Spain became one between the central and the regional forces as much as that between conservative and progressive ideas. Both the Basque and the Catalan regions – particularly the latter – have marked the transition through language laws and, significantly, through language use. Street signs, the language of education – including advanced education – and even the language to be used in airplanes of Spanish airlines serving Barcelona, must be Catalan: the impetus behind legislation and social or commercial practice of this type is clearly political and aimed at the creation and strengthening of regional identity in close association with regional political power.

Norway's politicians and cultural elite made language decisions for the emergent nation after its freedom, first from the Danes in 1814 and then from the Swedes in 1905 (Haugen 1976). Linguistically, the three Scandinavian languages are very close to each other: so close in fact that speakers of each in a three-way conversation can understand each other to a large extent. Politically, however, the situation is very different as speakers simply do not recognise that the three languages could form a whole, and certainly are not prepared to reduce the status of their 'national' language to that of a mere dialect. Within Norway, indeed, there are two standards: *bokmål* (book language), previously known as *riksmål* (national language) and *nynorsk* (New Norwegian), previously called *landsmål* (country language). The very names indicate the nature of the political language battle that has gone on over these linguistic forms, all of which are artificial in that they were deliberately created to respond to beliefs about Norway rather than about Norwegian. The first (*bokmål*/*riksmål*) derives linguistically from the four centuries of Danish control: it is written like Danish with a Danish vocabulary but pronounced with Norwegian sounds and is widespread now. The second (*landsmål*/*nynorsk*) still acts as the standard for about a sixth of the population and for many scholars and institutions: it is, in essence, a reconstructed form that is derived from rural, conservative, western forms. Politically, there is a strong preference for the rural dialects that are ethnically and nationally more 'real' – hence for the 'landsmål': however, in practical and economic terms the 'boksmål' acts as the official language.

Since 1989 and the liberation of Eastern Europe from Soviet control, language laws consecrating political control over language use have proliferated as new nations declare their special character and their desire to shake off the political power of the former Soviet Union and its official language – Russian. The demise of Russian throughout Eastern Europe since 1989 is probably one of the best examples of language shift for political reasons. Requests and demands to the World Bank or to European Union funds for the teaching of English have been almost as frequent as demands for western expertise in management education or transport. The massive growth of – sometimes dubious – trade conducted in English or German rather than in Russian is matched by the almost universal use of the dollar as the international currency.

The political rejection of a dominant language is by no means new: in Poland the First Partition of 1772, and the disappearance of Poland altogether as a political entity from 1795, brought domination by German and Russian, the languages of the partitioning countries (Austria, Prussia and Russia). From 1848

Polish had some political strength again, but only in the Austrian part of the 'German' area: the 'underground' Polish schools and the opposition to the enforced use of other languages led to language riots in 1901 in the Prussian area. After the First World War Polish was restored to the whole country, but the language itself had greatly increased in regional variation because the political divisions had had their effect. Indeed, this and the growth of other languages meant that in the 1931 census nearly one third of the population had a first language other than Polish. After the Second World War, with further political border changes, Polish became the first language of most of the population, and by 1989 only one per cent of the 35 million inhabitants had a minority first language.

Language shift: social factors
Social pull

It is common experience that those who wish to advance in society adopt manners of speaking that are those of what they regard as the elite, and that much social leadership derives from the ability to express oneself in such forms. This 'social pull' exercises considerable fascination and is one way in which individuals are attracted to manners of speaking that are different from those they knew in early life. In this way, language shift may be a phenomenon, not so much of communities as of individuals who demonstrate social mobility: adjusting and readjusting their language as they do their social role. To a certain extent this process is a part of growing up: adopting the language of adults and joining advanced society is a stage we all go through.

The process can be more severe than merely dropping childhood expressions and school slang in order to adopt the educated language of the advanced examination and the job interview: it can involve a wholesale shift towards a different language rather than just a different style. Usually the attraction is towards a language that has a more developed culture (French as opposed to Breton), or a greater social cachet (Dutch instead of Frisian – or indeed German instead of Dutch). This attraction may also apply within a linguistic community, towards a style of language seen as advantageous. Many young people may thus reject the standard language and deliberately adopt the slang and linguistic forms of the youth culture. In France, a marker of such attractiveness is the adoption of verlan or reverse slang, which, although its attractiveness may not last long for particular individuals, is remarkably persistent as a feature of French.

Social push

Account should also be taken of a 'social push' as well as a 'social pull'- the rejection of socially marked languages or social dialects by speakers who do not wish to associate with such groups. In this way social varieties may disappear as the elite, then the mass, leaves language forms which characterise non-prestigious social categories. It has been suggested that women looking for social advance for their children are prime movers in adopting standard forms and socially prestigious forms and in rejecting socially stigmatised language varieties. One of the best examples of the social push factor in operation is that of Spanish in the United States, where the general rejection of Spanish by the leaders of society has a whole range of social consequences. Mainly, these are concentrated on the availability of social-support mechanisms and mean that if the applicant cannot ask for welfare help in English, it may not be given – an excellent motivator for language learning! In Europe, there is a history of elites, usually aristocracies, abandoning their local languages, dialects or accents in order to adopt more prestigious forms.

The examples include the rejection of:

- Welsh by the Welsh gentry after the Act of Union with England;
- Breton in the sixteenth century;
- local forms of English by the elite and their replacement by either the non-regional, standardised forms of English or the 'posh' pronunciation (Received Pronunciation) disseminated by the fee-charging (and thus socially divisive) Public Schools.

Frisian speakers in the Netherlands are said not to prize their own language (Giordan 1992). Dutch journalists, when Frisian is mentioned at all, regard it as folklore – 'it's quaint' – and, if anything, mock its backwardness. There are examples of professional linguists who regard Frisian as an inappropriate language for public meetings or as a dialect without status. Politicians make public protestations of support, and there is a formal Pact between the central and provincial governments to maintain the language, but little in the way of practical policy. The general lack of enthusiasm for Frisian by its speakers is said to reflect a widespread language attitude in the Netherlands anyway.

This attitude is represented by four measurable opinions which seem to be generally shared by the majority of Dutch speakers. First, it is said that since Dutch is a minority language in Europe there is little point in expecting speakers of French, German or English to learn it. Second, its speakers expect to be bilingual or indeed multilingual in order to communicate – even within the country. Third, speakers of Dutch never insist on Dutch being used in mixed conversations and are ready to give it up straight away. Finally, speakers of the language have no pride in its correct use: they are ready to accept any approximation to the language by non-native speakers. These attitudes are said to be expressed to an even greater extreme by speakers of Frisian. Socially, the declared use of Frisian represents the classic case of a language that is little valued, and all the indicators of social value repeat the same story. In the province, 95% of the population is said to understand it, 75% can speak it, 67% read it but only 10% write it. Among workers, 69% can speak Frisian but the percentage drops to 29% in the higher professions. The social elite in the province is mainly composed of non-Frisian speakers: Dutch speakers, although in the minority, hold social power and are the decision-makers. Internal migration has brought about an influx of Dutch speakers as Frisian speakers have deserted the countryside for town life. Frisian is less and less the language of the home and is less frequently transmitted from parents to children.

There is however a counter to the rejection of languages by the elite in this way. Some social tendencies have been noted in research that suggest men in particular may deliberately retain local accents, and even dialectal forms, to stress their desire to belong to local groups: they often reject the standard language because they do not wish to be regarded as other than loyal to their roots. Regional, 'uneducated' languages may thus have an atmosphere of virility, of strength and of raw power that is attractive to those who wish to show that they have not become weak and effeminate despite having risen in the social circles. Studies of this covert prestige – the best researched example is that of the local variety of English in Norwich (Trudgill 1972) – are based on self-evaluation, when people in effect say that they behave in the same way as the group to which *they* look up, even if this is generally despised in society.

These social factors can be reflected in more general social processes such as social mobility. As social categories grow or decline in importance, so does the language they symbolise. Agricultural workers, for example, have decreased as a proportion of the population in many countries in Europe. As they disappear and their members become factory workers, they lose the need for agricultural vocabulary or the norms of the agricultural variety. Speakers of the agricultural variety no longer have pride in what they say or how they say it and they are unsure about whether the variety they speak is a 'real' language or whether its vocabulary has any 'real' existence. In this way, rural varieties become marginalised as the language of the country bumpkin. However, those who reject the rural variety may not yet feel secure in their mastery of the way city dwellers speak, so for a time – a generation – speakers are insecure and unsure of how to measure ways of speaking and how to ascribe prestige to them. This may account for much of the linguistic and social instability that has marked the twentieth century. Such social processes have been blamed for the disappearance of many dialects and, indeed, many languages. For example, Breton and Basque within France have suffered from the disappearance of rural society but also from mass conscription during the First World War and from the tradition of migration from the region towards Paris for socio-economic reasons (large families), to the extent that no monolingual speakers of either language remain. Of the 1.3 million native speakers of Breton at the turn of the century less than 25 per cent of the population of the province now retain some knowledge, and they are mostly elderly people, keeping the use of Breton as a form of social intercourse at home or in clubs. Intermarriage between populations is the inevitable consequence of contact, and although two parents with different first languages may have bilingual children, it is unlikely that such skills will persist into the second generation.

Language shift: economic necessity

The language of business

Generally speaking, economically necessary languages are attractive to language users while languages without economic value lose their attraction and may disappear. This is a generalisation that applies particularly at the present time to English, and to the use of any language other than English for commercial purposes. Commercial English is a *lingua franca* and as such is a reduced form of the language usable for its particular purposes and functions. These functions, at their lower levels, are very specific indeed: the description of goods, the documentation which accompanies the process of identifying goods and processes (brochures, pamphlets, advertising), ordering, purchasing, delivering and ensuring that finance is exchanged. Much of the language of transport – shipping, airlines – is also English of this reduced sort. At a higher level, however, two types of business language are involved: the language of negotiation, which is essentially spoken and is used in dialogue between two parties; and the language of legal contracts. Both of these are much more complicated than the first level, but nonetheless use fixed phrases, give a particular meaning or interpretation to certain words and sentences that recur frequently, and are limited to a particular type of vocabulary and grammar. Vehicular languages have not necessarily grown up by chance. Commercial English is widely used because the British Empire, followed by the Commonwealth, maintained English as a worldwide language and because the British generally followed the motivation that lay behind the Empire in the first place, that of trade and commerce. The United States is today the world's foremost economic power, and consistently uses English.

Governments have encouraged the use of commercial English: the design of Basic English, with its limited vocabulary and grammar, was intended to assist in the spread of English throughout the world. The creation of the British Council, and its support by the British Government, as we shall see later, were designed partly to ensure the spread of English both as a product in its own right and also as a means of exchange for commerce in general. The overall result of this economic pull factor is that English, or at least a reduced form of English, is now the most widespread foreign language in the world. It is spread partly by official educational systems, but also through sheer necessity: traders in Europe and worldwide just cannot avoid its use.

Economic changes: urbanisation and industrialisation

Stable rural communities are generally better at maintaining their (local) language than are urban communities. The latter tend to lose their original dialect forms and regional languages to adopt standard languages and linguistic varieties, since they are characterised by shifting populations. This generalisation depends on a number of factors, and may merely be a reflection of the modernisation that accompanies urbanisation anyway. As a region industrialises, rural communities leave the land and are grouped together – in factories and offices for work, and in estates, blocks of flats or individual houses for living – where the opportunities for the social activities reinforcing language use are reduced or at least fundamentally changed. These factors are not solely economic, and the economic factors themselves are often conditioned by the social pressures to which populations are subject.

Rhaeto-Romance (Romansh) is the language spoken in the Swiss canton of the Grisons and in two small mountainous areas of Italy, where it is known as Friulian and Ladin. In times when the mountain valleys were, in essence, cut off from each other, self-sufficient and saw little trade conducted outside the valley, the languages of these remote areas survived and indeed became differentiated from each other. The danger of eventual disappearance came, and comes now, in the main from German, and is primarily economic.

There are four main components. First, migration of non-Romansh speakers towards the Grisons. Second, migration of Romansh speakers away from the Grisons. Both of the first two are to a certain extent dependent on the infra-structural developments of roads and railways. The third component is the lack of economic advantages in the Grisons. This leads to commuting, short-time working or wholesale displacement of the Romansh-speaking community outside the area and to increased contact with German for economic purposes, and the force of this factor is dependent on the growth of urbanisation and industrialisation outside the canton. Fourth, the effect of media – press, radio, TV – in German on those who remain, coupled with the need to participate in social and political life.

By 1980 about 50,000 people still spoke this language in Switzerland – under 1% of the total population – although only some 30,000 of these were still located in the Grisons themselves, so migration away from the area has been considerable. In the Grisons, the 30,000 speakers are by no means a majority, and although the territorial principle holds in Switzerland and the harmonious linguistic relationships are held up as a model, there are continuous strains and Romansh is recognised as a national, but not as an official, language. Nonetheless, there had been only 47,000 Romansh speakers in the Grisons in 1835, so although the language has dropped considerably in 150 years, it is still used and still retains both numbers and status.

There are many other examples in Europe of the pressure economics applies to language choice. A factor in the potential death of a language is the migration that industrialisation brings: Italian speakers from Turin and from the southern part of the peninsula have migrated to the Aosta Valley in large numbers since 1950 as the valley became more developed, and French – the original language used in this border valley between France and Italy – has been used less and less as this has happened. In the Basque country in Spain, incoming speakers of Castilian have had considerable effect on the use of Basque for local administrative and educational purposes. In Wales, it was for many years the policy of supporters of the Welsh language, fearing for the future of Welsh and fully aware of the problem of migration by English speakers, to actively campaign against any influx, even to the extent of burning holiday cottages which would be used only for a short time in the year. English migration is still seen as a major danger (Jones, R. O. 1993).

Language attitudes

Behind these political, social and economic factors affecting the ways individuals maintain, drop or shift languages lies a complex matrix of language attitudes and feelings about language. Two particularly strong feelings are those of exclusion and inclusion. Xenophobia is an extreme form of exclusion. Hatred for foreigners is a symbol of refusing to accept that other ways of life might exist, and is realised by rejecting both the external markers of difference such as skin colour, religion, culture, history and language but also the less obvious indicators such as choice of vocabulary and accent. Xenophobia characterises many modern societies, and in language terms is often manifested simply as the rejection of borrowings from foreign languages, although it has many stronger manifestations – as in the theories of the National Front in Britain or, in particular, France. By contrast, elitism is an extreme form of inclusion. Identifying a particular social group within society as the 'best', as a group of people in some sense superior to others, encourages all members of the community to identify as closely as possible with them and to regard their language as the best, purest and most refined form. This is a social phenomenon most strikingly seen in the English reverence for Received Pronunciation, an accent taught and disseminated through the public (i.e. private) school system and estimated to be spoken in fact by under 5% of the population. Another prized group is rural speakers of older varieties of the language: many people feel that language is at its purest when it is spoken by those who represent the 'true ethnic heart' of the 'race', who have stayed close to the land, have not been subjected to the processes of modern industrial and commercial life, and have not been defiled by modern media and entertainment. So 'real' and 'honest' English might be spoken in rural Somerset.

Inclusion and exclusion are 'ethnic' feelings, but are often transferred to political communities and hence to official languages. Many States act as though it is their duty and their privilege to support and defend ideas of innate value and prestige in 'their' language, but sometimes confuse the standard and the official language. It may be for this reason that in the end the relationship between the State and language is tenuous and eludes the grasp of the politician, despite the array of Academies, legislation, defensive committees, publishers and the media many States erect in the vain hope of seizing advantage, and which we shall examine in the next Chapter.

The State and the 'official' language

The relationship between the political community, exercising its power through the State, and the linguistic, ethnic or other minority communities which exist within these political borders, yet do not themselves control the State, is inevitably tense. The 'ideal' – 'one race, one language, one State' – has only been expressed in such extreme terms by fascist Germany. In this chapter we aim to examine 'top-down' language planning by States who try to establish, maintain and protect the status of their official language, and to increase its status outside their own borders, noting that for many States the other ideals of fascism are anathema. In all cases it is the political community that decides, as a matter of policy. How this is done varies greatly from country to country, and indeed from time to time. It can be done without legislation as such, or through formal declarations, making language one of the symbols of the State along with the flag, or the national anthem.

Hungarian

Hungary, and speakers of Hungarian (Magyar), have found themselves at the centre of many European battles over official languages. Hungarian speakers are scattered over a widespread linguistic community, where political changes have meant that States have come and gone while speakers have continued to inhabit much the same geographical territory. Political borders have rarely coincided with those of language use. Many Hungarian speakers have found themselves firstly in States where their language was prized as that of the majority, then in successor States where Hungarian was the language of a minority, and sometimes in States where Hungarian was marginalised and all but persecuted. Hungarian may dominate; need to be protected; be decried and sometimes outlawed; be regarded as the symbol of political opposition or as a symbol of international solidarity.

The ancestors of modern Hungarians left the Volga plains about 1500 BC and spent some four centuries from the fourth to the ninth centuries AD, in the southern Russian steppes in close contact with Turkish and many other languages. They reached the Carpathians in 896 and settled in roughly their present area from the tenth century. A number of linguistic influences affected the language, which, since it is of the Finno-Ugric family, is quite different from its neighbours:

- Slav-speaking missionaries;
- translations of the Bible and other holy works in Latin.

- The use of Latin as a superior language in a number of domains such as Parliament, scientific and legal documents.
- Various languages used by the aristocracy of the regimes under which Hungarians have lived.

All have left traces of their influence on modern Hungarian. Protestantism raised the status of German; Catholicism that of Latin, and both languages have provided new vocabulary from which Hungarian has borrowed.

Hungarian power was considerable for six centuries. From 1000 AD Hungary controlled an ill-defined territory – roughly that of the former Roman Pannonia – stretching towards Poland, Bohemia, the regions under the control of Kiev and/or Austrian powers, and ruling much of the Balkans to the South including most of Croatia and a good part of Serbia. However, this power was based on feudalism, subject to constant wars which: increased Hungarian strength (in the twelfth century); demolished it (in 1240 with the Mongol invasion, in 1301 with the end of the native Arpad dynasty, and again with the growth of Habsburg domination) and refashioned it. As a result, the country contained, under the Angevin Kings in the 14th century, a huge range of languages, administrative systems and economic interests, with little logic or fellow-feeling among the constituent groups. Constant war with the Habsburgs, the Austrians, and the Ottoman Empire, led to the weakening of power, and control by the Turks for more than a century. The language rarely achieved political prestige, and its demise was even predicted in 1791.

The principal domination in the eighteenth century was by Germany in the Austrian Empire. It was during this century in particular that the ethnic and linguistic divisions of the Empire sharpened. Slav speakers and Hungarian speakers demonstrated a new-found sense of nationalism in riots and wars. However, the same demand for tolerance and understanding was notably lacking towards Romanian, Slovak or Serb minorities in these self-same regions. By 1867, after Prussian defeat of Austria, a double monarchy was created and the Austro-Hungarian Empire was born. Hungary, at this time, could be said to have become a fairly compact State with centralist traditions, favouring the assimilation of other groups.

Hungary became independent after the First World War and the Treaty of Trianon in 1920. The history of the defence of language rights, and the lack of them that the population of Hungary had suffered, meant that language debates and language laws were closely associated with political ideologies during both the nineteenth and twentieth centuries. The Hungarian State was reduced to the areas where Magyar was in the majority (it lost two-thirds of its pre-war territory): Croatia joined Serbia, Transylvania joined Romania and Slovakian regions were reallocated to Czecho-Slovakia.

Much of the language debate between the World Wars was for some, conditioned by beliefs that the Magyars had inherited the prestige of the Huns and the close association of language and political rights was based on a mixture of nationalism, racial purity and the desire to regain political control over the one-third of Magyar speakers now living outside the Hungarian State. The net effect of the political turmoil is that about ten million Magyar speakers live in Hungary itself. A further two million live in Romania; some five or six hundred thousand in Slovakia; a further similar number in the former Yugoslavia, in the Serbian province of Voivodina; some two hundred thousand or more in the Ukraine and a few thousands in Austria – not to mention the millions who have left Europe altogether and now live in the United States or Australia.

In all the European areas there remains considerable linguistic turmoil, with constantly changing language legislation, breached as much as obeyed, and associated with a mixture of persecution and opposition in a range of policy areas from housing to economic advantage.

It is against a background such as this, that linguistic legislation needs to be judged. In its more extreme forms, such legislation often tends to decree unity – that the State, the Nation, the people and the language are all one – and imposes a requirement that all citizens assimilate to this concept. In order to evaluate such legislation, commentators need to know:

- how coercive it is and what punishments are involved for infringement?
- From the point of view of the citizen, what (sort of) rights are conferred: is there a method for enforcing any rights which are granted?
- Despite the legislation, what is important is the implementation of the law: what is the situation in practice? Is there real imposition of language requirements, is there effective discrimination or protection, or is the law merely a symbolic declaration?

The Hungarian Nationalities Act of 1868, which started with the 'explanation' that all Hungarian citizens formed a single, indivisible and united nation, irrespective of the nationality to which they belonged, and that Magyar was thus the official language, is generally decried as 'infamous'. This is mainly because the penal code gave no remedies for citizen's rights and thus in effect relegated non-Hungarians to the rank of second-class citizen. Secondly, the code made it an offence to incite riot against any nationality having its home in Hungary. This could be interpreted as meaning that any support for local independence, autonomy or national/linguistic awareness was an attack on the Magyar nation, and led to a number of show trials against Slovak nationalists. Thirdly, the 'magyarisation' process by which the civil service operated in Magyar and, in effect, recruited and promoted only Magyar speakers, discriminated against, for example, Slovak speakers.

French

An example from more recent times is France. In 1992 France declared French to be the language of the French Republic, as one of the Constitutional changes necessitated by the Maastricht Treaty (Ager, D. E. 1996c). The debate which accompanied this declaration stressed the symbolic nature of the language, and the absolute necessity for France to place it on the same level as the other cultural symbols of what it meant to be French – the flag, the anthem, the slogans and descriptive phrases. Interestingly, the first formulation claimed 'French is the language of France', and politicians had hastily to reverse the formula to 'The language of the French Republic is French' when they were politely reminded by Belgians, Swiss, French Canadians and indeed many others, that the language was also used outside France. The symbolic declaration was given substance by a law of 1994, replacing one passed in 1975, but found to be ineffectual in safeguarding French, particularly in preventing the inflow of English words and expressions.

Previous legislation of 1539 had required French to be used in the Courts. In the laws of the French Revolution, French was also declared as the language of administration and of education. In fact, the 'Language Terror' imposed on Strasbourg and the German-speaking Alsace region in the early years of the Revolution, showed both how extreme some language laws can be – the requirement was that French alone be used by people who did not know the language and had never used it, and the punishment in some cases was death – and how language laws can symbolise political policies and attitudes. The logic was unassailable: the language of liberty, French, had to be imposed since opponents of the new regime intended to keep the populace in backwardness and ignorance by using the local German dialect. In this view, France itself could only be created through the common use of French. Hence, it was the duty of a Government to regulate language use, if necessary by force: freedom by decree.

The 1994 'Toubon Law', so called after its proposer, the then Minister of Culture, Jacques Toubon, decreed that French must be used in six main domains: education, commerce, the media, the workplace, public service and the conference industry. An officially approved vocabulary had to be used by public servants (who include all teachers, researchers and many workers in non-privatised utilities and industries). Civil servants' career prospects were to depend on their use of French and a supplementary Circular from the Prime Minister to all Ministers underlined this in April 1994. Punishments, ranging from fines to imprisonment, were to be levied on those contravening the law. Public debate at the time was generally in agreement that something should be done, despite accusations of Fascism, the despair of linguists about such misguided attempts to impose language use by decree, and a specific reference of the Act, by the Socialist Opposition in Parliament, to the Constitutional Council, to see whether it breached the fundamental principles of the Constitution. The decision was that any attempt to impose language use on the general public was unconstitutional, but that the Government had every right to require public servants to use French and there was nothing wrong with imposing quotas of French music on radio and TV stations, enforcing the use of French in colloquia or in advertising. Many British newspapers – and indeed some French ones had a field day chortling about 'Mr Allgood' (i.e. M. Toubon) and his ludicrous Law attempting to ban 'Anglo-Saxon', but few of them made any serious attempt to understand the motives nor the sense of offence many French citizens clearly felt about the take-over of their culture and way of life by alien influences.

The effectiveness of laws like these is certainly higher than it was in the 1970s and 1980s. The enforcing agency for the previous French Act quickly discovered it had better things to do than lay itself open to ridicule by conducting a vendetta against small-time businessmen, who had the temerity to label their car sales businesses 'Showroom' rather than using a French term. There were one or two show trials – of British Airways, for example – but these led to squabbles with the European Commission about free competition and a humiliating climbdown.

The Toubon legislation took the precaution of sounding out the Commission first, used the 1992 Constitutional amendment and the GATT negotiations on the cultural exclusion concession to get the Act through and made sure it could be presented as part of anti-American, pro-European legislation rather than simply anti-English. Nonetheless one of the first announced victims of the 1994 Act was a British firm, The Body Shop, fined in late 1995. The Commission has also been notified of objections in the case of insurance contracts, where both German and British firms have been obliged to draw up documents in French, even though their operations apply throughout Europe and they may have only minor interests in France. Overall, during 1994 the government organisation charged with identifying incidents, had investigated 1,918 cases, found 308 offences, issued warnings for 201 of them and transmitted 107 cases to legal officers. To judge by the outcome of the 165 cases transmitted in 1993, which had resulted in only 22 convictions, the effort is great but the results less so.

Switzerland and Belgium

At least two European States have accepted that they cannot, and do not wish, to achieve or defend monolingual official policies: Switzerland and Belgium (Siguan 1996, 69-75). In both these cases at least two languages are accepted at the official level for all purposes, although the practical outcome is different and there remain considerable difficulties. Both demonstrate clearly the importance of the territorial principle, and in both it is in practice possible for monolingual individuals to exist within defined parts of the country. In Belgium the present situation is a compromise outcome from a situation in which language has often been the symbol of conflict. In Switzerland, the equilibrium is harmonious and generally problem-free.

Belgium is a particularly complex country insofar as its linguistic communities are concerned. It was formed in 1830, and at that time French was the language of the elite, of power and of the government where the Flemish (Dutch) speakers felt themselves to be in the position of a weak, powerless minority. Since then, with increasing economic and political power, the Flemish community has gained power and independence, to such an extent that it is now the French-speaking Walloons who feel themselves to be in the minority position – and they are in fact only about 30% of the population.

There have been many Constitutional changes since the 1939-1945 War, and the position at the end of the 1990s is that the country has become a federation made up of the two main linguistic communities, each with a strong sense of its own identity, each with its own political structures and powers, but with a central Federal Government whose powers are mainly external. The Belgian Constitution establishes four linguistic regions – the Flemish, French, German and the bilingual region of the capital Brussels; and three linguistic communities – the French, Flemish and German. It had been intended that political and social powers would be split between communities and regions, and that the communities might be enabled to protect or support their speakers, even when these were located in regions where their languages were not in the majority. However, in practice the Flemish regions and community are one, and the practical rights of the German community and region are limited – education from the secondary level, for example, is normally in French or Dutch.

The four-language situation of Switzerland, and the harmonious relationship between languages and government, are often held up as a model for countries where language-related strife is common. The four languages are national languages, although Rhaeto-Romansh is not an official language as the others all are. The languages are spoken in fairly clearly delimited territorial zones, and it is the cantons which decide most matters connected with their use, in education, the law or political life. It may well be the existence of these prescribed zones of language usage which have avoided many of the problems of language-based conflict which have affected other States.

The German Community is by far the largest in Switzerland – some 73% or more of the population. The German-speaking region is also the richest. It includes the Zurich area where more than 10% of the Swiss population now lives and which is the base for most of the financial activities and power. Swiss German has recognised dialectal differences with standard German. However, the linguistic awareness of the Swiss population and their economic and political weight – they form some 5% of the total European German-speaking population – means that this dialectal form has considerable prestige of its own, despite its apparently inferior situation as a minority within the German speech community. French in Switzerland is nonetheless stable, and even sufficiently prestigious in Switzerland to allow towns like Geneva and Lausanne to resist the cultural domination of Zürich or even Paris. However, like German, speakers of the language are aware of its minority position within the French speech community, and also within Switzerland.

Italian is the third Swiss language in terms of power, numbers and political strength. Like French, it is in a minority in terms of the political control of the country, but unlike French, has no major town in the cantons speaking it, and is very subject to increasing immigration from Italy itself. Like French-speaking Switzerland too, the Italian part is very subject to domination by German-speaking Zurich, but it is the Romansh part of the country which demonstrates the problem of survival most clearly. Romansh is spoken in both Switzerland and Italy; has a long history in Switzerland of domination by German, represents only 1% of the Swiss population and only 39% or so of the population of the Grisons canton where it is centred. Pressures against its maintenance are strong:

- Even if the TV budget were allocated proportionately to the different language populations, this would account for such a small amount of air time that only 1% of transmissions would be in Romansh.
- The cost of translating all the official documents is prohibitive; all speakers have to be at least bilingual and can use Romansh only in minor domains and functions.
- Any social or economic progress for individuals, particularly if it involves moving, can only lead to less Romansh being used overall.

The State and the official language: defending a symbol with corpus policy

States protect the status of the official language by a number of means quite apart from the brutally simplistic one of passing a law to enforce penalties for not using it. Language Academies have long been set up to look at the actual language as it develops and to make sure that there is some official control or at least approval for new vocabulary. Some States control the language used in the media – often on the excuse that without such control the use of violent, sexually explicit or offensive terms would be widespread. This type of official approval is often very helpful to governments concerned at attacks on themselves, their own personnel, or on their own view of what society should be or on the business practices they regard as normal. Other States influence the dictionary makers, the editors or publishers of books and magazines, or provide subventions for professional associations of sub-editors or proof-readers. One should not exaggerate State influence in areas like these. In most European countries the publishing industry is completely free of State influence, and it is the general consensus of the industry itself that maintains language norms, in much the same way that the speech community does. However, the opportunity for political control of speech, and hence of thought, is never far away from actions such as the establishment of a preferred terminology for a subject area, or official approval for the expressions to be used in sales and employment contracts.

Language Academies

The French Academy, by far the best known of the European language Academies, is by no means the first or even the most effective. Set up in 1634 as an informal gathering of interested courtiers, its potential and value were quickly identified by Cardinal Richelieu, and its formal constitution was approved by the Paris Parlement the following year. Ever since then, it has been a meeting of forty 'Immortals' from literature and the arts, inevitably elderly and rarely expert in linguistics. One of its purposes was to standardise the language; another to 'render it capable of expressing the arts and sciences and becoming a satisfactory instrument of Government'. It set to work with a will and published its first Dictionary in 1694. It soon discovered however, that there was little hope of achieving agreement on the more complex areas of style or literary form, and gave up attempts at regulating these. It made no specific attempts at regulating administrative language, either. Over the years it has published new editions of its Dictionary fairly regularly, including spelling corrections and changes in them, but it has had much less success with its attempts at defining grammatical accuracy: its most ambitious attempt at a grammar of the language published in 1932 was howled down by professional linguists and it has perhaps wisely left the field to commercial publishers since.

Nowadays, the Academy sees its role as being that of following usage, rather than of determining it, and until recently did not see itself as an arm of Government. Indeed it had been on more than one occasion, critical of what it saw as excessive Governmental action in attempting to dictate what should be said or how the language should develop. It opposed recent language reforms, on sexist language, on spelling reform, and was more or less ignored in the debates over the Toubon Law. But since then, and because it is generally venerated as a respectable part of the Establishment, it now oversees the job of regulating scientific and technical terminology.

The first of the European language Academies was probably the Italian Accademia della Crusca, set up in Florence in 1582-3. Its first dictionary was published in 1612, and its role today remains much as it always was – a centre for language research – and although it played a role in the determination of standard Italian in 1862, the formal recommendation then, was made by a specially appointed Commission under the leadership of the author Alessandro Manzoni.

The Royal Academy for the (Castilian) language was set up in 1713 in Spain. Unlike France, it was set up so that its membership included linguists and philologists, who could thus enable it to be an authoritative body, and its pronouncements on language are generally regarded with respect. In Germany the seventeenth century saw the foundation of a number of language societies. The most important was set up in Weimar in 1617, and concerned itself with attempts to rid the standard language of dialectalisms and to decide on matters of correctness. It also dealt with borrowings from other languages and with the proper role of archaisms. However, Germany was a country of small princedoms until unification in the nineteenth century, so none of the societies was really able to take on the role of authority for German.

Other Academies were established for Hungarian in 1825, Romanian in 1879, Basque in 1918 (but without legal status until 1972). Sweden did not get its Academy until 1786, although the idea had been mooted in 1652. Britain nearly got one in 1712 after a petition to the Crown by such figures as Jonathan Swift, Pope and Congreve, but for some reason – and the authorities are unsure why – it was not set up, and the British Academy, although it has interests in a range of cultural matters, is mainly known for its work in painting and for its role supporting Humanities research generally.

Academies suffer from the fact that they are generally ineffectual: if they contain prestigious citizens, such citizens do not wish to follow political priorities and if they do not contain prestigious citizens they have no effective voice. They are often purist and see language change as equivalent to corruption and decay. Their strengths and weaknesses reflect their innate but necessary elitism and conservatism.

The control of terminology

Academies are often ill-suited to devising or gaining acceptance for the terminology of a scientific area or for agreeing the sense to be given to words and expressions in legal documents, or in new technology. For these purposes some European States have set up official language offices or give government support to research centres in the expectation that they will set up Terminology Banks or specific translator support mechanisms with a range of approved terms.

France has thus established the Délégation Générale à la Langue Française, one of whose main jobs is to co-ordinate the work of Terminology Commissions in each Ministry and provide specific technical assistance as required. These Terminology Commissions set up an agreed list of the meanings of certain words or expressions. These were arrived at after a lot of consultation and debate among representatives of the Ministry itself but mainly with the relevant industry and occasionally with the consumer groups. The resultant list – often not very long – is published as an official Ministerial order, and the terms must be used. However, since the decision of the Constitutional Council in 1994, such Terminologies are not binding on the ordinary public and although occasional publicity is given to words like baladeur to replace Walkman, or bogue to replace (computer) bug, their fate in the general language is open to doubt. From the point of view of the Government, the purpose of the Commissions is to propose French words to replace English borrowings. But the Commissions' proposals are open to criticism by linguists. Some terms are imported along with the referent and there hardly seems much point in searching for new terms, when it is the object itself that is perhaps objected to (English 'spot' replaced by bande promotionnelle); some proposals do not cover the full meaning of the original (parrainer to replace sponsoriser). Others have been absorbed into the language and have often lost any meaning in their original language (clip), while some really do not need a Ministerial Commission in order to come up with what is proposed (disque compact, boumeur). Some linguists conclude that the whole exercise is pointless; others that such language management is essential to the future independence of the language and the society that uses it. It must be said that much of the impetus to do this sort of work in France derives from the experience of Quebec, where the need was perhaps greater and certainly different from that of France.

The unofficial language planners: mass media, dictionaries and all that
Newspapers are often condemned as being full of jargon, as containing examples of the worst excesses of language play and the greatest attacks on the 'proper' corpus of the language. Examples abound in almost any language of ways in which journalists telescope information, give a new twist to reality, shock and startle their readers, and push the language to the edge of understanding. The publishing industry, too, is responsible for the language, although in a rather more considered and long-term way than the media. Its copy-editors, type-setters and manuscript readers are rarely identified, rarely specifically trained for their job, and seldom able to come together in professional associations or other fora. They carry out much of the task of keeping published books accurate, comprehensible and acceptable. Such unofficial language users are the arbiters of taste and even in countries like France, with a strong tradition of State control, it is only at arm's length that interference takes place – for example through consultation over language reform proposals like the spelling reform of 1990 (Ager, D. E. 1996c).

The State and the official language: protecting a symbol with educational policy
Gillian Shephard, speaking to the Conservative Party annual Conference in 1994, spoke about the pride citizens should feel in the proper use of their own language:

> It's our heritage. Not only is it the tongue of Chaucer, Shakespeare and Milton, it is now the language of the world, uniting continents. And here at home why should anyone expect to get a job if he or she can't speak or write clearly in our marvellous language. I shall use my time as Secretary of State to campaign for the use of plain, simple, effective English – not just in the classroom, but in the media, in industry and commerce, even in Parliament.

She is said to have been surprised by the response to her speech – numerous letters were published in the Press and many comments sent to the Department. So much had she found a subject which could provoke a response, indeed, that she repeated her speech the following year – almost word for word. It is not surprising that it should be a Minister of Education, who found herself in the role of linguistic expert. Education policy requires there to be a definition of language correctness: teachers must agree on what is acceptable and examiners must be prepared to decide when a pupil's use of the language exceeds the licence allowed to creative artists. Britain has only recently adopted a National Curriculum, but a component part of this is an official, Government-approved language policy which specifies for the first time, the forms and types of exercise, teaching style, tests and language which will be acceptable. This has come about after fierce battles with teachers and educational experts, and is still not altogether accepted as being the job of Government. Educational policy in France is even more prescriptive. From time to time, the Ministry publishes a list of the departures from orthodoxy which markers may accept – in spelling, grammar and style – and both the programmes for individual subjects and the marking schemes examiners have adopted for school subject examinations are approved and published by the Ministry.

Spreading the official language outside Europe: winners and losers.

There have been two main modern periods when European countries deliberately tried to establish their hold over countries and continents outside Europe:

- the fifteenth to the seventeenth centuries, with the discovery of international trade, and the division of the world by the Pope between the two main colonial powers of the time, Portugal and Spain.
- The nineteenth century – particularly the period between 1871 and 1914 – when the rush to colonise Africa represented the height of imperial Europe and all the Great Powers except Austro-Hungary – Britain, Germany, France, Italy and Russia – tried to ensure advantage for themselves.

Colonisation and settlement have ensured the spread of European languages outside the strict confines of the original country. However, there are other influences, and there is no doubt that the motivations of European States for supporting the use of their language outside their borders are now very mixed.

In the 1990s, Mandarin Chinese is spoken by some 850 million people world-wide. This is followed by English with about 450 million, Hindi, with 363 million, comes next, followed by Spanish with over 300 million speakers. Russian has a similar number, while Arabic has over 200 million speakers; Bengali nearly as many; Portuguese about 150 million; Japanese 130 million; German 110 million and French about 100 million. Italian has about 60 million speakers (Ager, D.E. 1996a, 44). These statistics are very approximate. They do show however, that European languages are widely known, and, unlike Chinese, Hindi or Bengali, they are known to, and used by, those for whom they are not a maternal language. How far do the European States see it as their duty to propagate and defend 'their' language world-wide? And how far is this still possible?

Portugal

Portugal was one of the first maritime nations to seek riches across the world. In the fifteenth and sixteenth centuries Bartolomeu Dias, who rounded the Cape of Good Hope in 1487, Vasco da Gama, who opened the route to India in 1497, and Cabral, who took Brazil in 1500, showed how adventurous they were. The Treaty of Tordesillas of 1494 divided the world between Spain and Portugal, and it is thought that Portuguese sailors probably discovered Australia. Portugal also established an overseas Empire.

Brazil was first colonised in the sixteenth century, and Portuguese had to compete there both with a lingua franca derived from indigenous languages, and with the Creole African slaves developed (Baxter 1992). Interestingly, the lingua franca was prohibited from official use in Brazil in 1758, and Brazilian Portuguese started to show significant differences from the European language during the eighteenth and nineteenth centuries. There remain today some 170 indigenous languages in use, plus a number of European languages apart from Portuguese spoken by groups of immigrants both new and old. Brazil became independent in 1822, and codification of the Brazilian forms of Portuguese – particularly in spelling – was undertaken by the Brazilian Academy which still approves standard dictionaries. Brazil's population of 130 million far outweighs that of Portugal (some 10 million), and the language is considered to be the national one, so there is little continuing influence from Portugal itself. Indeed, Brazilian Portuguese is fast becoming the main international form of the language – principally through a major export trade in soap operas for TV. There are linguistic differences between the Portuguese and Brazilian forms, although in most cases Portugal and Brazil have agreed to adopt the same forms, and there are continuing attempts to do so through a common Language Council.

Portugal first colonised African areas in the sixteenth century, and today five States use Portuguese as their official language – Angola, Cape Verde, Guinea Bissau, Mozambique and São Tome and Principe. These did not finally achieve their independence until 1975 and the language they used until that time was officially the Portuguese of European Portugal. Since then they have gone some way towards changing the status of the indigenous Creole. As with other African ex-colonies, the European language exists in a multilingual environment, and with the decreasing importance of Portugal on the world scene, Portuguese itself is to some extent giving way to international languages like English – due to the nearness of South Africa to Angola and Mozambique – and French. Indeed São Tome and Principe, and Cape Verde, have joined the international 'Francophonie' organisation made up of French-speaking nations and regions. Nonetheless Portuguese retains the major role in the media. The role of Portugal within the European Union gives former colonies access to European money and influence, so that African countries are sometimes torn between Brazil or Portugal as their model, despite the general unwillingness of Brazil to play a major role on the international scene, and the inability of Portugal to play a major financial or military role.

Spain
The effect of the Spanish discovery and exploitation of Central and Latin America is well-known: not merely did it ensure that the potato would be the staple diet of many Europeans, but it introduced venereal diseases – Montezuma's revenge – and the possibly worse evil of rampant inflation as Latin American gold wrecked Spanish wealth. However, far more significant in its long-term effect, the Spanish language is now widespread and is fast becoming the second language of the

United States of America. Spanish is today spoken in more than twenty countries, including, quite apart from Spain itself and the United States of America, Argentina, Bolivia, Chile, Colombia, Costa Rica, Cuba, Dominican Republic, Ecuador, El Salvador, Equatorial Guinea, Guatemala, Honduras, Mexico, Nicaragua, Panama, Paraguay, Peru, Philippines, Puerto Rico, Uruguay and Venezuela. The language is the second most widespread European language after English, and is significant, not merely in that its use represents the legacy of a major Empire, but also that it has become the main, if not the sole, language of the countries where it is used. Spanish is not merely a language of the elite in former colonies, as is the case with French, but is the language of the whole population and as such has developed urban vernaculars and popular varieties outside Spain. The distribution of Spanish also means that, although there are two main varieties – the Iberian (Castilian) and the Latin American (for which Mexican is usually regarded as the norm), many countries develop their own norms and there is enormous inherent variety in pronunciation, vocabulary and usage. The Royal Academy in Spain works with numerous Academies or Language Councils based in the other Spanish-speaking countries despite these differences.

Interestingly, Spanish is the second language of the United States, and as such is entering a period of direct conflict with English. A number of the States have already declared English to be their official language – a sure indication that there is some doubt that it might be – and with the growth of immigration it is already difficult to live in the United States without at least some knowledge of Spanish. Use of the language is fast becoming a declaration of social status – Spanish is the language of the underclass – and one must expect that before long there will be attempts to ensure a reversal of the current greater prestige of English. At that point, the whole basis of the United States will be brought into question.

France

At an early stage French sailors, fishermen, settlers and pirates spread French to North America, the Caribbean, India, islands of the Indian Ocean, and to Africa (Ager 1996a and 1996c). The early expansion was followed by setbacks: France lost considerable areas as a result of the collapse of the first Empire in 1760. It retained a foothold in Madagascar, Mauritius, Réunion and the Caribbean (Martinique, Guadeloupe, Saint-Domingue (Haiti) from which came much of the wealth of some leading members of the French government. Later, Napoleon conquered most of Europe and the Middle East, but without establishing lasting colonies. During the nineteenth century France expanded into North Africa – Algeria was conquered in 1830, although battles continued until 1847; the Pacific, with Tahiti and French Polynesia, Wallis and Futuna, and New Caledonia from 1840, although French settlement of New Zealand and Australia was prevented by prior claims and brute force by the British. In Africa, from 1852 to 1865, France expanded from the North, the South and the West to conquer an immense empire, bigger in this continent than that of the British. In 1840 treaties were concluded with the

Vietnamese Empire to modernise their armies, but the second and third opium wars of 1856-1860 led to an easy military conquest of Saigon, followed by the establishment of protectorates over Cambodia and six Vietnamese provinces. At the turn of the century the Union Indochinoise was established: 740,000 square kilometres, 10 to 11 million inhabitants, covering present-day Vietnam, Cambodia and Laos.

There are now speakers of French in all the continents. The French used in European countries other than France – Belgium, Switzerland, Luxembourg and the Aosta Valley – is subtly different from standard French, and these frontier regions do not share fully the attitudes, vocabulary or preferences of the French of France. Francophone Africa is normally multilingual, with French only one of a number of often competing languages, and each language often has defined functions and particular uses. French is often an elitist, minority language, a vehicle for science, technology, commerce and diplomacy. Depending on the country and its history and situation, a version of French may however be in popular use – for example in the Ivory Coast and Senegal. French is in any case part of the multilingual mix of Africa, confronting not merely local languages but other exogenous languages as well, particularly English.

The contemporary situation of Quebec, where French and French-based values are in conflict with English, and of Guadeloupe, where the continuation of conflict is based on a battle with the locally developed Creole, illustrate the conflicts French faces. Quebec has suffered rejection since the 'repatriation' of the Canadian Constitution from Britain in 1982. In 1980 Quebec had rejected complete independence from the rest of Canada by 60%-40%. The 1990 failure of the Lake Meech accord, between the Federal and Provincial Prime Ministers to resolve Quebec's demands, and of the 1992 referendum on the Charlottetown agreement on the Constitution – which had been carefully prepared by numerous Commissions and a massive public relations exercise, but which was nonetheless rejected by 54.4% of the electorate and by six of the ten Provinces – led to a hardening of Canadian Anglophone attitudes towards possible autonomy for the province.

Economically, there is not much doubt that Quebec, whose Gross Domestic Product is bigger than that of Denmark and as big as Belgium's, could exist independently. Politically, the internal problems – with the native peoples, immigrants and other groups, and particularly the nature of the relationship with the rest of Canada – mean that independence would not necessarily solve all the difficulties. However, the 30th October 1995 referendum, which Federalists won by 50.6%, did not quite produce independence, although it seems almost inevitable that this will come at some stage. Then Quebec will become an independent, French-speaking country in North America, as de Gaulle had hoped in his provocative speech in Montreal in 1967. Quebec has affirmed its language rights in increasingly strong terms: the province is monolingual and the range of language defence mechanisms placed in position to defend Quebec's right to use

French represent the most complete legal mechanism for the protection of a language minority anywhere in 'Francophonie', which has often served as a model to France in developing its language laws. Nonetheless, the danger of being swamped by English is still present: if 67.2% of new immigrants used French in 1986, 72.4% of them also used English.

Guadeloupe is a good example of an area in which the sociolinguistic situation assigns different roles to standard French, to Creole and to other languages. Linguistically, Creole is the normal language of Guadeloupe, with standard French in the official role, in education and in administration. For the French Government in Paris, Guadeloupe has no other language than this official French since the Département is an integral part of the French Republic. The ethnic mix of the population is 80% descendants of slaves, 10% originating in south-east Asia, 5% 'Creole Whites' and 5% from France, mainly administrators posted for a tour of duty. As elsewhere in France, it is only recently that citizens have any rights to use a language other than French, and, indeed, the 1994 Toubon law insisting that French alone be used by public servants may well have the effect of ensuring that administrators and population become even more alienated from each other.

The conflicts between French and other languages across the world are really of three types:

- Indigenous languages in conditions of societal bilingualism in dependent countries like Guadeloupe or independent African countries, where sometimes French is a symbol of power and domination and sometimes a symbol of opposition.
- English, for world dominance or competing influence, as in Quebec.
- Arabic – as in North Africa – with Flemish – as in Belgium – or occasionally with other languages, where French symbolises a set of social structures, values or identities which conflict with those conveyed by the other language.

The French belief in the universality and importance of French cultural values for mankind could be seen even during the time of massive colonial expansion in the nineteenth century, when it was possible for official figures to say 'We affirm that the work of colonisation of the Third Republic is fundamentally one of civilisation', and to note that 'Our colonies will not be French in mind and spirit until they understand French...Particularly for France, the language is the necessary instrument for colonisation' (quoted in Ager, D. E. 1996a, 12). This attitude has remained consistent, and although French is widely disseminated it has not varied or developed local varieties which might act as regional linguistic or cultural norms. The role of Paris is still predominant and deliberately fostered by France: of all the French speakers in the world, more than half live in France, and it is inevitable that Parisian French and the cultural, social and political values of France will dominate. From this point of view it is possible, somewhat unfairly, to allege that Francophonie still represents a form of European intellectual domination[1]. Some consider that this is continuing even in international organisations like the Francophone summit meetings, where nearly 50 countries or regions meet to debate the advancement of Francophone interests. Certainly France itself provides massive support for its language and for cultural diplomacy. French is seen by the French authorities to be a worthwhile item for cultural export, and there is heavy subsidy both of the international Francophonie movement which ensures media collaboration between French-speaking countries and also of organisations like the Alliance Française, whose purpose is to undertake French language teaching (Ager 1996c).

English

The winner among the European languages in terms of its international and widespread usage is however clearly English (Burchfield 1994). Although there are political and commercial reasons for this there are also linguistic reasons. English is particularly noticeable for the ease with which it borrows and incorporates words from other languages. Its vocabulary is after all a mixture of Germanic and Latin roots and it borrowed massively from French until the fourteenth century. English is a comparatively easy language to learn: no complicated morphology and a fairly straightforward grammar. English speakers are tolerant and they are quite happy to make efforts themselves in order to understand a pronunciation which is not that of southern England. They are also prepared to accept approximations to grammar and style by learners or second-language speakers who have retained quite a lot of the preferences, rhythms and pronunciation characteristic of their own original language. The varieties of the language found in Australia, New Zealand, South Africa, India, the United States or Canada are both understandable to speakers of each and also not tied to any one centre for ideas of perfection: there is a norm for each of these speakers. Indeed there is much discussion about whether the various forms of English used over the world are one language or many: American, Indian or Australian types of English, as opposed to American, Indian or Australian Englishes. But particularly important is the fact that there exists an 'international English', a reduced form acceptable for international negotiation in any domain and which is widely understood.

Australian English derives from the many dialects spoken in what was at first a convict settlement mixing people from a wide range of social and regional origins. The particular characteristics of the variety rose from this mix and from such features as contact with Aboriginal languages or the specific experience of living in a vast, varied country where the flora and fauna, the agriculture and even the industry, differ from those of the country/countries of origin. New words like kangaroo, dingo, wallaby, billabong, boomerang entered the language to describe new realities; existing words and expressions like magpie, walkabout, referred to different realities. The extent of such vocabulary and the frequency of its use should not be underestimated. It very quickly becomes obvious to any visitor to Australia that words like tinnie, creek, station, barramundi and yabby are common parlance.

The effect of Maori words and linguistic habits on New Zealand English dates from James Cook's notes on his circumnavigation of the two islands in 1769, when he claimed the country for the British. The influence of Maori on New Zealand English is particularly strong in vocabulary: place-names, often somewhat adapted from the original Maori, are used (Waitangi, Whangarei, Rotarua); many New Zealanders use pakeha for a non-Maori; kauri (a tree), kiwi, kumara (sweet potato), poi (ball used in dancing), hangi (celebration meal) are terms in general use. However, there are many other influences, too: the Scottish settlement in South Island, the Anglo-Catholics in Canterbury, the Devon settlers in North Island, Irish immigrants to South Island in the 1870s and 1880s, Australian gold-seekers in the 1860s, constant immigration from Britain – particularly the South – until very recent times, and, slowly, Asian and Pacific immigration for the last twenty years or so.

In South Africa, English came up against two major linguistic groups which have affected the development of a specific norm: Dutch – or its South African variant Afrikaans - and the number of Khoisan/Bantu languages spoken by the original inhabitants into whose lands both white groups moved during the nineteenth century. It took until the Act of Union of 1910 for both English and Afrikaans to be accepted as official and the struggle between the two traditions has had numerous consequences. For example the Soweto riots of 1986 which were fired, among other things, by the obligatory use of Afrikaans as a teaching medium in African schools. The country is still widely bilingual in these two languages at an official level while the speakers of African languages are necessarily often multilingual. Of the 35 million or so of the population, about 10% are English first language speakers, 25% Afrikaans speakers, 17% Zulu and another 17% Xhosa. There are of course in South African English a number of vocabulary items, coming mostly from Afrikaans, with particular South African connotations – stoep, kopje, kraal. Some words derive from the political or social situation, and may also relate to a particular time – apartheid, Kaffir, township. South African English has a specific and recognisable pronunciation, marked by short vowels. Such differences from the British norm are striking enough for it to be quite clear that the richest country in South Africa, as it develops its wealth and political power, will develop also its language practice and if it retains English, confirms its use at the official level, and develops its use as a national lingua franca, may have major effects on international English as such in the future.

In South Asia and the Indian sub-continent the contact English had with the local peoples again produced a recognisably different standard variety of the language, if not two. The differentiation between Indian and Pakistani varieties of the language has become more marked in recent years, and it may well be that the political independence of Bangladesh will produce yet a third. In any case the vast numbers of English users mean that 'beneath' these standard languages there is an enormous range of varieties, conditioned by the nature of the transaction, the interlocutors, their knowledge of the learned language and a range of other factors. English has survived since the time of British domination in spite of modern Indian language policies aimed at countering the effect of Lord Macaulay's Minute of 1835, which deliberately introduced English into education throughout the sub-continent and hence attempted to create people 'Indian in blood and colour, but English in taste, in opinion, in morals and in intellect'. The effectiveness of this piece of social engineering cannot however be disputed. Indeed, Indian authors and publishers make India the third largest English-language book producers in the world. Even in average size cities there is an English-language newspaper and radio and television make widespread use of the language.

As an Indian language, English is part of a complex multilingual mixture: it is nearly always learnt as an additional language, it is a pragmatic language used for specific purposes and since it is learned in the educational system, its pronunciation often imitates spelling. One of its main characteristics is the stress, rhythm and intonation of its pronunciation, another is the complements (for enjoy reading, enjoy to read) while yet another is the widespread isn't it? tag question. A large number of words have entered sub-continent English and indeed many have become widespread in standard British English: bangle, bungalow, curry, dungarees.

The United States and Canada are the real powerhouse of international English, however. The economic and political strength of the United States means that it is impossible for traders or diplomats anywhere in the world to have no knowledge of American English. The United States of America, gaining their independence from Britain in the late eighteenth century, originally depended on immigration from Britain. However, the massive immigration from Europe and farther afield, which took place in the nineteenth and early twentieth centuries, has had major effects on English and on the relative prestige in which different languages are held. Such publications as Webster's 'American dictionary of the English language', appearing in 1828, established an American norm, accepting spellings like color and center. Although some linguists consider that the only differences between standard American and standard British English appear in some spellings, in vocabulary (pavement, hopefully, fall, faucet, suspenders) and in some phrases (I'm missing you already), there is little doubt that Americans agree that their language is identifiably different from British English. American in the United States has developed internal dialect differences, most notably between the North and the South, but also – and this has been specifically recognised in recent years for reasons other than linguistic ones – with the development of Black English varieties.

The Caribbean has nothing like the economic strength of the United States, and it is probably in the islands of the area that English has developed farthest away from its British norm, to the extent of creating a Creole which is often extremely difficult for speakers of the English or American standard to understand. There may be some impact of such Creole on British English in

Britain, although it is not maintaining its former strength or separateness within immigrant communities in the British Isles.

Overall, English – particularly its American form – currently dominates international relations in significant areas, in technology, trade and diplomacy. It is widespread as a native language; it is the most widely learnt foreign language, and its role as second language is unsurpassed. Britain supports the business of English language, which is a major earner for publishing houses, although not for the Government, which has set its face against deriving financial or cultural benefit from such a trade and no longer supports work by the British Council in this field. There is much greater support for cultural diplomacy and for the English langugage, from the US government (Phillipson, R. 1992).

Pidgins and Creoles

International English is a sophisticated form of a contact language, a linguistic pidgin. Originally, pidgins were also called trade languages: they developed from the necessity to trade in areas of the world where no common language existed. Pidgin languages were, as contact languages, limited to one domain of use: the business in which they were useful – selling goods, giving instructions, passing orders. Most developed from English, Dutch, French, Portuguese or Spanish and traditionally used the grammar of an African or Pacific language and added the vocabulary of the European one, developing to the status of a Creole as they became mother tongues. Most are now used outside Europe, particularly in areas of the world which were previously colonies, or which continue as dependencies of European nations: French overseas Départements such as Guadeloupe or Martinique, British colonies such as the Bahamas or former colonies such as Jamaica maintain such Creoles and they are much used by immigrants to European countries. They pose a number of linguistic problems for the educational system: should the Creole be taught? should it be eliminated from the speech of immigrants? should it be maintained as a marker of (ethnic) unity? Creole usually has a low level of prestige in European countries, so decisions such as these have considerable effects on the self-value Creole speakers can have. European countries do not generally support Creoles, and prefer to spend money supporting the official, standard language rather than such variants.

Notes

1. 'The French believe, with all their being, that there exists a human truth, belonging to everybody, which can be comprehended by intelligence and expressed by (at least the French) language'- quoted in Guillorel 1995, 334.

Language, the State and the regional community

Regionalism

In this and the next Chapter we investigate multilingual political communities. Usually, these are made up of a majority speech community and one or more minorities, which may be territorially based or spread throughout the population. The majority community may be an ethno-linguistic community; most minority communities declare themselves as such. Usually, too, there is opposition to the State and to its official language. The opposition may take a number of forms, be violent or peaceful, be conducted in political, social or economic fora, be led by individuals or be the result of mass movements. In most cases, however, opposition is directed at the State, as the supreme political structure, and this is usually associated with conflict between the majority and minority community/communities.

We are concerned in this chapter with territorially-based, regional minority languages spoken within political States, that is, a language could be a minority in one State even though it may be the majority tongue in another. German is thus a regional minority language in Belgium and elsewhere, even though it is the majority language of Germany. Jews, Gypsies – Romany peoples – and many more recent immigrants, although indeed forming minorities within many States, are rarely limited to one geographical area and are therefore considered separately below when we examine the question of migration (Chapter 5). Within the countries where regional minority languages are spoken, bilingualism may be either individual, so that individual people are capable of expressing themselves and understanding more than one language; or societal, where individuals can remain monolingual and just not know or use the majority language as well as the minority one (Edwards 1996; Hamers and Blanc 1989).

Defining a linguistic regional minority is however not quite so simple as this. The basic criterion is that of the territorial principle, but there are at least four other meanings to the terms which help to explain why opposition to the State and/or to the majority is so widespread:

1. There is the obvious meaning: a minority is so because has a smaller number of speakers than the majority language in the State (e.g. Welsh in Britain).
2. Even if numerically a language is spoken by a majority, it could lack political power within 'its' region or even in the State overall. The traditional example is that of the

powerless languages in a colony, but a European example is that of the Flemish in Belgium – numerically in the majority since the inception of the State, but without political dominance until recently.

3. The term 'regional minority' could be limited to those who at some previous time in history formed their own political community and ruled their own destiny – as in Scotland, for example.

4. The term, finally, could be limited to those groups who have a subjective awareness of a separate identity and a desire to maintain it. Notable examples where such an awareness has led to active violence are Northern Ireland and Corsica.

Regionalism, the subjective feeling of difference by a minority within a political community, is rarely based solely on language or even on ethnic difference. There is always a complex of differences and problems between 'peripheries' and 'centres', between minorities and central authorities. Most of these have to do with economic and political problems. The peripheries of States are typically poor, backward, badly supplied with infrastructure (transport, educational and social facilities) and are located far from markets or finance. They are often sparsely populated, their political representation is insufficiently targeted to their needs, and always subject to the fact that their representatives have to move physically to get to the heart of power and, frequently, are seduced by this self-same power into making not merely a physical but an emotional leap away from their roots. Differences are often social and cultural, too: religion may be different, the tradition and way of life of the periphery is not that of the centre, the 'imagined community' to which the periphery belongs is not that of the centre. Due to the overriding difference between periphery and centre, many of the more traditional contrasts of civil society may be overridden as regional protests mount: the extreme Left combines with the extreme Right, industrialists share farmers' protests, the young are enthused by tales of the heroism of their forefathers. Some regions represent or contain an ethnic minority different from the majority in the State, use a different language and have different traditions and sense of belonging.

Although we have separated the geographical regions from the migrant communities in this book, very similar feelings often inspire the attitudes and actions of both minority groups and indeed the reactions of others to them. In particular the strength of feeling, the desire to belong to a distinctive group and to oppose other groups, should not be underestimated. Although violence is not a necessary component of regionalism or of ethnicity, opposition often takes violent form as the actions of some Basques, Bretons, Corsicans, some Northern Irish, Chechens, some Algerians in France and some Welsh, Blacks and Asians in Britain have shown.

To a certain extent regionalism, like motherhood, is a fact of life, and complete unity – one land, one people, one language – is impossible. So tensions between regions and States are to be expected. In some cases they are managed without major problems: in most cases they lead to some social, economic and/or political difficulty, both for the minority itself and for the majority. In extreme cases they can destroy the State.

European regions and regional languages
Spain

The generally recognised regional languages are Basque, Galician, and Catalan, and of these Europeans generally hear most about the problems of Basque, as in the following newspaper extract:

> **Basques light fires in streets**
> City centres have become a battleground, as militant separatists recruit disaffected youth to spread terror and destabilise society. The Guardian, 7.2.1996. (Translated from *El Mundo*.)

The article reports the level of violence in the Basque country between January and October 1995. During this time there were: 5,539 demonstrations, 5,000 of them unauthorised; 422 police reports and 104 arrests. Jarrai, the youth organisation of the radical left, was reported to undertake open protests in the streets on a regular basis. ETA, the radical separatist organisation, continued to wage a campaign of destabilisation, demanded amnesty for prisoners and carried out numerous terrorist acts. Within the separatist movement both political Left and political Right are represented. Some commentators say activists are fascist, others that they are Left-wing, others that they are merely skinheads, hooligans and extremists conveniently grouping themselves under the Basque national flag. And yet the organisation of Spain since Franco's death has ensured that Basque politicians run their own autonomous region; the police is Basque and locally recruited, prominent members of the Basque Socialist Party have been Ministers in the Madrid government. Despite these changes, the strong regional feelings continue and are associated with continuing opposition to the centre.

The Basque language has an illustrious history, as a unique language isolate having no known relationship to any other European language. Spoken by two to three million people, its seven regional varieties or dialects (eight according to some experts), are fairly distinctive from each other. A Basque Academy was founded in 1918 and the language has a standardised version taught in the schools both in Spain and France, although much work remains to be done on disseminating and perfecting this. Language policy in the Basque region is heavily orientated towards promoting education, although the task of teaching the language to non-natives is particularly difficult, and the overall position is that more than half the population does not speak or understand the language. The political history of the region reflects its independence, suppressed during the Franco period but with a respectable history since Roman times, while its economic history and present situation shows the increasingly negative effect on language and on social identity of urbanisation and modernisation.

Basque is not the only regional language in Spain around which separatist movements have coalesced, or which is recognised by formal agreements with the Madrid government. Catalan, like Basque, has a long history of conflict with Castilian. Spoken by at least 6 million, 17% of the Spanish population – and also by some 200,000 in France and a small number in Andorra and Sardinia – Catalan has been much influenced by Castilian. It acted as the symbol of regional sentiment, particularly through the Franco period from 1939 to the new Constitution of 1978. Catalonia has the major city, Barcelona, as its capital, and a developed form of local government, strongly protective of its identity and special nature. The linguistic symbolism is much in evidence: street signs, airport signs and even spoken public announcements are in Catalan. There is a fierce protectionist movement, considerable investment in language matters and education policy strongly encourages the use of Catalan, so that knowledge of and use of the language increased from 80% to more than 90% of the population between 1975 and 1989. The language is widespread and is in formal official daily use; in effect, Catalan is the majority language within its regional area. Television channels in Catalan also spread the language and ensure it is modern and relevant to everyday life.

Galician is spoken in the north-west, near Portugal, by about 3 million people and has a number of similarities with Portuguese although it has adopted fewer Arabic imports than either Portuguese or Spanish. About 40% of the population is said not to understand or use the language in the provinces involved and the speakers of the language are said to be mainly rural. Sociolinguistically, the language situation is one of diglossia with Castilian occupying the main public and official domains. As with Catalan, a deliberate policy of revival since 1978 is having considerable success in strengthening the role of Galician. As in Catalonia, the public authorities are concerned to raise the status of the language and strongly encourage its use as a medium of instruction in education, in television and the press. However, as there remains much local opposition to its more widespread use, the language is still in danger of disappearance. As with Basque, its use and particularly its standardisation, provoke fierce internal battles among representatives of different sub-regions, advocates of moderation or revolution in keeping or rejecting Castilian terms, and advocates of linguistic purism fighting the modernists prepared to bring the language up to date.

France
Breton, Basque, Catalan, Occitan, Corsican, German, and Dutch are all to a certain extent used as regional languages in France, in addition to the many languages used within the overseas possessions in the Caribbean, the Indian and the Pacific Ocean – formally part of the French Republic. France, however, is an excellent example of a European country which has pursued for more than two centuries, a policy of linguistic homogenisation which has entailed, as the counterpart of the high level of prestige accorded to standard French, a similarly high level of

oppression, ignorance or refusal to accept the regional languages as having any official or public value (Ager, D. E. 1990 and 1996c).

The fundamental choice was made in the French Revolution, when centralisation of the State was agreed and when the central role of education and of (the French) language as the route towards freedom was established. From that moment on, regional languages were regarded as symbols of backwardness, of counter-revolutionary feelings, or of the oppression of the population by aristocrats or foreigners. Individuals were deemed to make a social contract to become part of the Nation and there were to be no privileges or separate rights for any group of people. Legal decisions have since all confirmed the simple fact that the French State does not recognise the existence of minority communities, so Corsicans cannot be described as the 'Corsican people'. The 'one and indivisible' French Republic can have only one official language and its administrators, teachers and bureaucrats can use only French in their official role.

Nonetheless, there have been and are, growing concessions to the use of regional languages, for example in education. By 1996 students could offer most regional languages within the baccalaureate, including some languages intended to help the otherwise difficult situation of the overseas dependencies in the Caribbean or in the Pacific Ocean. Much effort by intellectuals, pressure groups and even through violence, has been expended in attempting to impose the use of regional languages, to encourage such use, or to force the State to accept use in various symbolic ways – on cheques, road signs or Social Security forms – all with little success. The French State makes little finance available for the general support of its regional languages. Sociolinguists and political commentators have been interested to note how support for regional languages forms part of the politicians' range of promises, but is rarely followed by action. Mitterrand's period as President was ushered in by a number of promises of support, but it was generally felt that the Socialists had done little to put these into action during their 15 years in power. The regional language question is closely associated with the problem of regional devolution. After the passage of a law in 1982 giving the regions formally elected assemblies, budgets and a set of responsibilities decentralised from the Paris government, much of the ferocity has left the regional economic and political battles which languages often symbolised. Violence nonetheless continues in Brittany and Corsica, and extremists continue to hope for complete autonomy.

Great Britain

Welsh and Scottish Gaelic are the two regional languages best known and best supported in the United Kingdom. Both are, now, well supported by the central Government and Welsh has even achieved the status of an official language in all but name in Wales, where it is accorded the same level of validity in legal proceedings as English (Ager, D. E. 1996c; Grillo, R. 1989).

Indeed, the strengthening of the 1967 Welsh Language Act by a new Act in

1993, and the concomitant establishment of a Welsh Language Board with powers to compel public bodies to institute schemes for the use and support of Welsh, together with the allocation of reasonable funds for the language, make Wales a very favoured country compared with the regions or countries within most superordinate States in Europe. Welsh language use is reasonably well established – about 20% of the population of the Principality is said to use it regularly – with a still higher proportion of young people familiar with the language. In schools its use both as object of education and as medium of education is established through the National Curriculum, and most aspects of the education service have a recognised Welsh dimension. Without going so far as the Quebec experience, and without having anything like the same resources available, the Welsh Language Board is likely to achieve very similar results in stemming the gradual disappearance of the language and in reintroducing it into significant areas of public life. What is missing, by comparison with the Quebec experience, is any deliberate attempt to ensure that private business uses Welsh as an internal language to any significant degree, and the massive Quebec investment in linguistic matters such as corpus research or aid for translators to identify and use agreed terminology.

In Northern Ireland many of the Nationalist and Republican groups have associated Irish with other symbols, in particular the tricolour and the special place accorded to the Catholic religion, as an indication of their desire to join the Irish Republic where Irish has been the official language since 1922. However, in practical terms it is said to be used by no more than about 25% of the population. But in Northern Ireland the language plays little practical role and its special significance is as a symbol for political views, so Sinn Fein conferences, for example, display posters and banners in Irish.

Italy

Article 6 of the Italian Constitution requires the Italian Republic to 'protect linguistic minorities by appropriate laws'. Nonetheless, specific actions to protect the eleven or so minorities have generally only come about, since 1946, either by international agreements or through international pressure. The first case for the recognition of language rights is that of the German-speaking minority in the Trentino-Alto-Adige and in the South Tyrol regions, where a specific Italo-Austrian agreement led to a semi-official status for the language and its speakers, agreed in the late 1960s for about a quarter of a million speakers. Secondly, there is the 1970 status for the Aosta Valley, where a French-speaking minority of about 75,000 continues to use French and its representatives have observer status at the international meetings of Francophonie, the French equivalent of the Commonwealth. The third case is the status of the Slovene-speaking minority around Trieste, which was agreed with the then Yugoslavia in 1977 for about 100,000 speakers. In fourth place, about 30,000 Ladin speakers in the province of Bolzano also have special status. These four territorial minorities clearly use languages other than Italian, but as we have noted above, Italian dialects are often markedly different from each other and the national language, in effect the Tuscan dialect, has only relatively slowly become practically used and available to all.

Politically, two of the three regions have developed regional political parties whose aim is further independence for their regions: the Union Valdotaine in the Aosta Valley and the Südtiroler Volkspartei in the South Tyrol. There are at least two other large minorities which exist wholly within the Italian State and which have been somewhat less well protected. These are: the million speakers of Sardinian living on the island, and the half million Friulians, whose language is in effect the same as, or very close to, Ladin and the Rhaeto-Romansh of Switzerland. Other minorities are often the result of twentieth-century immigration (Albanian, Croatian, Greek) but some represent communities remaining after much earlier settlement (Catalan, Occitan).

Greece

As in most European countries, territorial linguistic minorities are mainly found near the frontiers of the State. Because of history, too, it may well be that the State is not too concerned to identify such minorities as separate communities, nor to encourage them to maintain their separateness. This lack of enthusiasm for difference often extends to not collecting language-use data in censuses. Indeed, when the data is collected, since it depends on self-definition, it may well be that many people do not wish to identify themselves as too different from the State to which they may wish to assimilate, and they thus under-report the size of the minority group. The last language census in Greece dates from 1951, when of the total population of some 7,632,801, there were 92,219 Turkish speakers, 41,017 speakers of Slavonic 'Macedonian', 39,855 speakers of Wallachian, 22,736 Albanians, 18,671 speakers of Pomeranian, 8,990 Armenian speakers, 7,429 Gypsies and various other smaller minorities – for example 1,218 Sephardic Jews speaking a form of Spanish (there had been more than 60,000 of these in 1928). The Turkish speakers, remaining after the Treaty of Lausanne of 1923, which itself put paid to massive population movements between Turkey, Greece and Armenia, and the general association of language with religion, represent the nature of one of the 'problems' associated with language minorities in Greece.

Greeks are defined as belonging to the Orthodox religion and the Constitution recognises the special role of religion in the definition of the unique character of the Greek nation. The only recognised minority with specific rights is the Muslim population whose rights were defined in the 1923 Treaty. Greece itself, like other Balkan nations, emerged from the Ottoman Empire during the nineteenth century. It became an independent country in 1830, and one of the tasks of its governments was to create a sense of nationalism among a very diverse population. The myth of Ancient Greece, the unifying power of the Greek Orthodox Church and the development of an artificial language to act as the new national symbol contributed to this sense of nationalism. This artificial, literary language –

katharevousa – was indeed only replaced as Greece's official language by the more popular variant demotiki in 1977.

Macedonia is perhaps the central point where the new Balkan nationalist constructions of the nineteenth century and later confronted each other. Macedonia lies where the Greek, Serbian, Albanian and Bulgarian national spirits coincided, and the problem of identity this conflict encouraged remains a major difficulty today. For example, it has led to violence in such far-away places as Australia where 'Greek' and 'Macedonian' communities burnt each other's churches in 1994. Macedonian is a Slavonic language, and for Greeks, those living within Greece are merely Slavophone Greeks. However, the long history of the 'Macedonian question', dating back to the partial withdrawal of the Ottoman Turks from the Balkans in the nineteenth century, involves not merely language but also religion (the Macedonian Church was long unrecognised by the Greek Orthodox Church), international relations (Macedonians are divided among many countries) and symbolism (the fight over the right to use the name 'Macedonia' continues apace).

It is hardly surprising that the sensitivity of the situation surrounding minorities and their definition, the religious question, the relationship with other States and a strong sense of history, have led to a feeling that for the central government to accept the rights of minorities as such, can only lead to the destruction of the State and of social cohesiveness. The State lives in fear: for its stability, for its territorial and geographical identity, for the continuity of its values, and the force of its spirit. In this sense, the Greek State regards minorities as enemies, and makes its opposition to them known.

The Czech and Slovak Republics

Czechoslovakia, formed after the first World War, combined mainly two peoples and languages and eventually split in 1992 to form two Republics. But the two mutually intelligible, main languages – Czech and Slovak – and the Czech and Slovak Republics are situated in the middle of a part of Europe where the hazards of history have found it very difficult to draw clear frontiers, where migration has relocated speakers often far from the concentration of their speech community, and where there is little logic about the formal situation of language speakers within the political community as it has evolved.

It is in the Czech Republic of about 10 million people, that the majority of industrial development has been located during this century. The Slovakian area of 4.5 million traditionally concentrated on a rural economy but was rapidly industrialised until, by 1990, it produced as much as, if not more than, the Czech Republic. Near the borders with Germany, particularly in the Sudeten area, many German speakers provided Hitler with his stated excuse for invading the country in 1939, and despite the length of time since, the conflict between German and Czech speakers is still present. This situation is hardly helped by the knowledge that the nearly three million Sudeten Germans were forcibly expelled in 1945, no matter how long they had lived in Bohemia, and that the Czech Republic will not have them back unless they are prepared to re-establish themselves on a permanent basis and adopt the official language of the Republic. This experience means that German and Czech are both in situations which share the characteristics of majority as well as minority speakers. The Germans are numerically inferior and thus feel themselves to be in a minority, but also have the feeling of being part of the European majority associated with the mighty German speech community, while the Czech speakers are apparently in the numerical and political majority but feel dominated by this self-same external German-speaking majority.

In Slovakia, too, the feeling is similar but even more extreme. Slovakian speakers who were in the minority position in relation to Czech speakers, are now in the majority in their own country, but are still in the inferior position in relation to both Czech and German. They do have many linguistic minorities that they could dominate. One of these is made up of the speakers of Rusyn (also known as Ruthenian, and found in the Ukraine, in Poland, Hungary and Serbia), a language only recently codified and standardised by a Language and Cultural Institute founded in 1993. However, the main Slovak linguistic minority is made up of Hungarian speakers, and there is a strong Hungarian influence on the Slovakian way of life. Indeed, the chequered history of the area means that German or Hungarian have often dominated; now Slovakian does, and mindful of this the Republic is aware of its linguistic minorities and conscious of the need to ensure their contentment. But although the Constitution itself guarantees many rights to linguistic minorities, the State retains the right to protect its own language in ways which decrease the rights of such minorities, as the following quotation indicates:

> On Wednesday evening, the Slovakian Parliament passed a law on Slovakian despite the protests of the Hungarian minority (600,000 strong, some 11% of the population) and those of Budapest. The text of the law requires the use of Slovakian for all official purposes, reversing the previous situation allowing Hungarians to use their language in towns where they formed more than 20% of the population. (AFP.) (Libération, 17.11.1995.)

Russia and the former Soviet Union – the minority languages

Chechenia has become famous in recent years due to the ferocity of its battles with Russia. This battle is only one of the many which have racked various forms of the Russian State since the time of the Tsarist Empire. Indeed the linguistic situation within Russia and within the former Soviet Union, is fundamental to an understanding both of the problems of building a sense of Nationhood during the Stalinist and Communist period and to the nature of the collapse since 1990 of the former Soviet Union, which has been a mixture of rejection of Communism, rejection of Russians and assertion of national independence. In 1783 the North Caucasian insurrection against the encroaching Russians was led by a Chechen; there were rebellions during the 1920s and 1930s; accused of collaboration with the

Nazis, the entire population was transported to Central Asia in 1944 and history was rewritten as though they had never existed: their languages were outlawed, their lands settled by imported colonists, maps were re-drawn to remove them. They were not allowed to return until the late 1950s and ferocious battles still continued in 1996 with Russia and with neighbouring Republics over the return of their territory. It is perhaps hardly surprising that the Chechens have the reputation of being the Mafia of the region and indeed of making up the major crime networks in Moscow.

As the Russian Empire, and the Soviet Empire which followed it, grew, Russian was inevitably to be the lingua franca and the second language for all who aspired to social and political progress. But there was always an awareness of the diversity of peoples and the fact that their identity would have to be reflected in special arrangements for their languages. Formed in 1922, the Union of Soviet Socialist Republics consisted of 15 Union Republics, 20 Autonomous Republics, 8 Autonomous Regions and 10 National Areas. According to the 1989 census there were more than 80 recognisably different language groups, and even among these 80 some were simply lumped together – for example, as 'Peoples of the North'. Republics were created on the basis of their linguistic and ethnic nationalism, even in the case of those closest to Russian itself. Thus Ukrainian would be the basis for the Ukrainian Republic, and White Russian would be the language of Byelorussia: both Ukrainian and White Russian, although for many linguists they are merely dialects of Russian, were accepted as different enough from the lingua franca to form the basis for political differentiation.

The 1989 census measured a number of aspects of the language situation in the Soviet Union, and there is no real reason to doubt the accuracy of the figures (Knowles, F. E. 1993). One interesting statistic is the percentage of the national group which declared itself loyal to its own language. Of the 80 language groups mentioned, all but 10 gave figures of more than 50%, with the highest being Russians themselves, followed by Turkmenians, Tuvinians, Uzbeks, Georgians and Chechens. Those showing the lowest figures of less than 50% 'loyalty', and thus being most prepared to shift language – usually towards Russian – were the Koreans (49.4%), Germans (48.8%), Karelians (47.8%), Greeks (44.5%), Czechs (35.3%), Finns (34.6%), Persians (33.2%), Chinese (32.9%), Poles (30.5%) and Jews (11.1%). Most of the speakers of these languages, however, were immigrants from the relevant countries, and most speakers would have been dispersed through the population centres. Despite the enormous size of the Soviet Union and the fact that the official language of most of the constituent Republics was not Russian, nearly one in two Soviet citizens claimed to know some Russian, and the extent of language shift towards this prestigious language was highest in these same dispersed and immigrant groups; again, only 1.7% of the Chechens declared that Russian was now their native language. Russian speakers themselves are dispersed throughout nearby Republics, mainly as a result of deliberate socio-economic policy during the Soviet period: six million in Kazakhstan; 2 million in the Baltic States; 11 million in the Ukraine. Currently, these Russian-speaking groups are often in some difficulty in the newly independent Republics as their former majority status is removed.

Estonia, Lithuania and Latvia, the three Baltic States, achieved their independence in 1918 after being dominated within the Russian Empire from the end of the eighteenth century. Before this their mainly rural populations had been under the sway of Swedish, Polish or German aristocrats and landowners. Independence – for example, for Lithuania in 1991 – came about only because of the collapse of Soviet power. Confusingly, the newly independent States are now discovering linguistic minorities within their borders whose status is unclear and who, in the case of the Russian speakers established in the country, as a result of industrialisation, are as dominated as ever the Lithuanians themselves were. Among the other linguistic minorities in Lithuania are the Tatars (some five thousand) – Sunni Muslims whose right to be in Vilnius goes back to their settlement in the fifteenth century after their defeat within the Golden Horde; the Karaites – descendants of former palace guards, and who now number no more than a couple of hundred. Groups like these can only with difficulty be satisfactorily offered any formal status, and to recognise their language for official purposes is practically impossible. Latvia and Estonia, too, are struggling with the consequences of large Russian-speaking minorities, many of whom are not themselves ethnic Russians but have adopted the language as a lingua franca.

European Charter and Convention for Regional or Minority Languages

A Convention for Regional or Minority Languages was accepted by the Council of Europe in 1992, although France, the UK, Cyprus and Turkey abstained and Greece voted against. In 1994, the European Parliament adopted the Killilea Report, whose provisions included further recommendations both that the Convention – the legal form of the Charter – should be signed by all European States and that the Commission should increase its activity in the language field. The preamble sets the tone of the Convention, stressing both the positive contribution of minority languages, the lack of danger they represent to official languages, and the need to consider the question in the light of Human Rights:

> **Preamble, European Charter for Regional or Minority Languages** (extracts)
> The member states of the Council of Europe signatory hereto,
>> Considering that the protection of the historical regional or minority languages of Europe, some of which are in danger of eventual extinction, contributes to the maintenance and development of Europe's cultural wealth and traditions,
>> Considering that the right to use a regional or minority language in private and public life is an inalienable right...,
>> Stressing the value of interculturalism and multilingualism and considering that

the protection and encouragement of regional or minority languages should not be to the detriment of the official languages and the need to learn them,

Realising that the protection and promotion of regional or minority languages in the different countries and regions of Europe represent an important contribution to the building of a Europe based on the principles of democracy and cultural diversity within the framework of national sovereignty and territorial integrity . . .

The Charter went on to recommend specific governmental action in relevant fields. It is fairly clear why the two main non-signatories – France and Britain – did not subscribe to the Convention. Both object that the Charter is at the same time too vague and too prescriptive, and does not altogether apply to their own circumstances. France is very wary of the notion of discriminatory laws, particularly when its own legal provision provides no status for regional languages but does by contrast very firmly assert the legal status of the national language. Britain has more precise concerns in relation to the Northern Irish situation, where it fears that the implications of acceptance might be to affect the status of particular communities within the province, and to give rights to which other communities might well take exception. Whether, in the fullness of time and with the growth of European political integration, the Charter might become acceptable to all; whether, indeed, its very existence indicates a possible alternative direction for the European Union in constructing a Europe of the Regions rather than a Europe of the States, only time will tell. In 1996, such a resolution seems very unlikely.

Language, the State and migration

Nationality, ethnicity and citizenship

Generally, the 'State' can be defined as an independent and sovereign political entity, although the creation of Federal and supra-State organisations like the European Union somewhat modifies the absoluteness of such independence and such sovereignty. A 'Nation', by contrast, has been defined as a 'group of people who feel themselves to be a community bound together by ties of history, culture, and common ancestry. Nations have objective characteristics which may include a territory, a religion, a language or common descent ... and subjective characteristics, essentially a people's awareness of its nationality and affection for it' (Kellas 1991, 2).

An ethnic group is more narrowly defined and relies on common ancestry: one can join a nation (by adopting its cultural attributes and subscribing to its self-awareness), but not an ethnic group. 'Nationalism' and 'ethnocentrism' are both an ideology and a form of behaviour, based on a favourable attitude towards one nation or ethnic group. They imply a negative attitude towards other nations and ethnic groups, but these negative attitudes when pushed to the extreme become xenophobia and racism. Somewhat confusingly, while 'ethnicity' is the state of being ethnic or belonging to an ethnic group, 'nationality' usually defines the fact of belonging to a State, which in democracies, where sovereignty resides in the people (France, Italy), is equivalent to the essentially political concept of 'citizenship'.

Europe's remaining monarchies (Britain, Spain) are 'constitutional' – even where the Constitution is unwritten, as in Britain – and although sovereignty resides in the elected Parliament, people are not 'citizens' but 'subjects' of the Monarch. Britain is also unusual in that Parliament contains unelected legislators in the House of Lords.

The basic division between two types of method for granting nationality/citizenship, is that between the place where one was born or resides and the nationality of parents: land and blood. People have nationality in the first case if they live in the territory of the Nation, while in the second case, wherever they now live, they belong to the Nation if they or their ancestors were born there. These two fundamental approaches – the territoriality principle and the personality principle, or the jus solis as opposed to the jus sanguinis – are rarely found in the raw state and most European countries have modified or adapted them in some way. The classic examples are Germany, where the concept of blood and origin is the main decider, as opposed to Britain, where the concept of residence is supreme. France has a specific concept of adherence to the social contract and the 'idea' of the Republic.

In Germany, those who can, at some point or other in their ancestral chain, demonstrate the existence of 'German blood', are entitled to full German nationality. Many of those whose ancestors left Germany – some of them in the Middle Ages – to settle in Poland or the former Soviet Union can and do return and claim citizenship as Aussiedler (Resettlers). In Britain, it is those who reside in the country who form the electorate, whether or not they are British citizens, so the electorate includes for example Irish, Commonwealth and European Union citizens (the latter for local but not national government). The list is amended every year, and citizenship rights include not merely voting but also access to housing, finance and legal aid. This territoriality principle is added to by a special list for electors now residing overseas, but who can claim links with Britain.

The French concept of citizenship is based on the association of nationality and membership of the political community, the State. Rousseau's ideas on the social contract, implemented in the French Revolution, added to residence in the territory of the State, the idea of voluntarily adhering to its beliefs and values, so the Nation and the State were the same: nationality implied citizenship. It took until 1980 before the first law on immigration (as opposed to Ministerial circulars or administrative decisions) was passed, and the difference between law, applying to citizens and guaranteeing rights, and administrative orders – or indeed the practice of local administrators such as the police or housing officials – applied to non-citizens, and guaranteeing no rights at all to such non-Nationals, is fundamental to an understanding of French treatment both of foreigners and also of immigrants.

Europe has known successive waves of internal migration during all its history. In the late nineteenth and twentieth century, internal, inward and outward migration have all increased. Internal migration has been affected both by the movement of communities and also by the redrawing of State boundaries, which have both created national and ethnic minorities within political States. Migration from former colonies towards the ex-colonial powers has created internal communities – particularly in the Netherlands, France and Britain, while German has known a more social inward migration. Massive outward movement from all over Europe towards the New World was particularly striking at the beginning of the twentieth century, establishing European communities across the world.

Non-territorial communities and migrant languages

An early example: Gypsies

Although Gypsies have a language – Romany – and a long history of centuries of persecution, their origin as a people is from North India. They are widely distributed throughout Europe but particularly numerous in Central and East Europe, and their collective national awareness remains the reason why pleas and calls for help are constantly addressed by organisations representing them, to international organisations like the United Nations (Liégeois 1992). Gypsies arrived in Byzantium in about the eleventh century, and in Western Europe during the 14th and 15th centuries. Many were forced to settle and so stayed in Hungary, Romania and Bulgaria, the area of the Ottoman Empire, although others moved West and North. Persecution – the death penalty merely for being a nomad – was normal in France, Prussia, the Netherlands, Italy, the Scandinavian countries, and indeed in the twentieth century in Hitlerian Germany. When they survived, the alternative policy applicable to them was in some cases the equivalent of slavery, in Romania, Austria and Spain.

The contemporary equivalent of these policies is based on opposition to the nomadic way of life and the need to document citizens. The practical result in most cases is to deny Gypsies the very characteristics which give them their identity. In view of this consistent history of persecution over centuries and the continuing generalised hatred and dislike of this marginal group, it is surprising to note that Gypsies are still present throughout Europe and that the estimate of their number is of the order of anything from three to eight million. Over two thirds are probably still located in Hungary, Romania, Bulgaria, Slovakia and the former USSR and Yugoslavia. But how could their ethnicity be recognised in modern circumstances?

Recent reports to the European Union suggest that the Gypsy communities themselves take the lead, although it is clear that there is no one Community: there are at least three major language groups and very rarely physical contact between countries. However, the dilemma remains: the essence of being a true Romany is to refuse society in its normal forms. If Romany culture is to be maintained, society must set aside its normal rules and differentiate between these and all other citizens. It must somehow differentiate, too, between 'proper' Gypsies and those who merely wish to avoid social rules. Defining Gypsy culture is immensely difficult: they have intermarried, absorbed many of the characteristics of the societies in which they live, from language to religion, and probably the only remaining common features are the strength of family ties, the concept of defilement, and devotion to the dead. It is unlikely that the dilemma of choice – absorption and hence disappearance as against separateness and hence discrimination – will disappear.

France

In 1921, immigrants formed 3.9% of the population, in 1931, 6.6% (Ager 1995). By 1954 the figure was 4.1%, in 1975, at the end of the post-war period of economic expansion and at the start of the oil crisis, 6.5% of the population was of non-French nationality. However, by 1982 the figure was still 6.8%, and it remains at approximately the same proportion now. As in many European countries, it is difficult to see the reality behind such figures. Some immigrants have assimilated completely, while others have retained almost complete separation from the host community. The problem is particularly sharp in France since the question of nationality and citizenship is fundamental, both to the statistics and to the reality of the situation. In 1990, the raw numbers of those retaining foreign nationality was 3.6 million of the total population of some 56 million, although the debate about immigration in France makes use of any of the following numbers: 2.9 million – those of foreign nationality born outside France; 1.3 million – those who have acquired French nationality, but were born outside France; 700,000 – those of foreign nationality born in France; 70-100,000 – the annual rate of 'new' immigrants; 5 million – the children of immigrants and another 4.4 to 5.3 million – the grandchildren of immigrants. Of course, if one goes far enough back, everybody is an immigrant!

Immigration has been a feature of industrialised France for many years. Immigration after 1945 was welcomed and actively sought to rebuild the country, and also, to maintain the flexibility of labour, keep wages down, enabling larger returns on investment. During this period, formal agreements were made with the sending countries and illegal immigration outside these agreed systems positively encouraged. Immigration stopped in 1974, when economic circumstances had changed. Since that time in particular, the social consequences of bringing in mainly single, male workers, and expecting them to return docilely to their homes when they were no longer needed, have been more and more the concern of the public authorities. Concern is directed most at the large population of those from North Africa, who are regarded as most difficult to assimilate.

In terms of raw numbers, such 'Maghrebins' account for about two million immigrants who have retained foreign nationality, of whom the majority are Algerians. By contrast, the largest numbers from any one other country are the Portuguese (about 650,000) and the Spanish, Italians and Turks (about 200 – 250,000 each). Political discussion has associated the Maghrebins with:

- The Gulf war of 1991, during which many of these immigrants supported Sadam Hussein.
- The Creil affair of 1989, where young Muslim girls insisted on wearing headscarves as a sign of religious belief while at school, which is traditionally a lay organisation and a fundamental symbol of French Republicanism.
- Political problems in Algeria, where election results were cancelled in 1992 as the Islamic fundamentalists were about to declare victory, and there have been many murders and other incidents since, including the hijacking of an Air France plane in

December 1994.

Immigrants generally have low economic and social standing. Seventy percent of those with foreign nationality are in unskilled employment. The unemployment rate of those with foreign nationality is nearly 20% as against 10% for those with French nationality. Most foreigners live in working-class suburbs of large towns, forming for example 12.9% of the population in the Paris region and 10% in Alsace and the Rhone-Alps. People with foreign nationality generally have larger families: 3.15 children on average per woman in 1982, 2.81 in 1990, as against the national average of 1.8. First generation immigrants, whether or not they are foreigners, are in general poorly educated, and women in particular often have little knowledge of French. Knowledge of French is very variable across the generations. In 1993, 43% of a sample of 500 aged 18-30 said the child in the family spoke French while parents spoke Arabic or Berber, in 35% of cases all spoke French and in 20% all spoke Arabic or Berber (2% no reply).

Since the Revolution, France has prided itself on the belief in universal human rights – liberty, equality and fraternity – in a secular, just society of emancipated individuals as put forward in the 1794 declaration of the Rights of Man and the Citizen, deliberately ignoring the Rights of groups and minorities and concentrating on the individual in his social contract as part of the Nation. Immigration can thus only be tolerated if it accepts the strength of the French identity structure, based on and around the myth of territory (the geometrical hexagon), of individual acceptance by the citizen of his role in defending the universal values of human rights, of the specific French contribution to humanism, and of the special role of the French language in representing these values. It is therefore hardly surprising that France welcomes immigration very little, nor that in the current debate on the matter voices in favour of integration and assimilation are heard more than those favouring the maintenance of separate identity. France has very few policies supporting language maintenance, for example.

Britain

As for France, mass immigration to Britain is comparatively recent, with mainly an economic motivation (Ager 1996c). Immigrants were sought to increase the workforce, and came from certain well-defined areas of the Commonwealth in succeeding waves: from the Caribbean, from Hong Kong, India, Pakistan, and some other areas of South-East Asia. As in France, the oil crisis of 1973 and its consequences brought the period of economic expansion to an end, and further immigration was supposedly restricted to family re-unification. According to the 1991 census, those members of the population in residence whose place of birth was not the UK totalled 6,925,368 or approximately 12% of the total of 58,039,416. Britain has an approach to nationality which is based on residence in the country. Hence one of the census questions asks respondents to indicate, not their own nationality, but the (ethnic) group to which they feel they belong, with the results that the statistics show a strange mix of ethnic group and country of origin.

51,810,555 residents declare themselves as 'White'; 840,255 as 'Indian', 493,339 as 'Black Caribbean and 208,110 as 'Black African'. Those of 'mixed origin' are 'black/white', 'Asian/white' or 'other mixed'. Despite these strange categories, immigrants have come mainly from ex-colonies or other possessions, and immigration to the UK is principally from the Indian sub-Continent.

During the 1960s, government policy aimed at dispersion and pursued a general hope of assimilation. A Department of Education and Science circular in 1965 estimated that the maximum permissible proportion of immigrants in one school should be 'about one third'. Over the following twenty years policies have moved towards integration, although three types of language maintenance schools, some with and some without financial support from local authorities or the State, help to maintain difference:

1. Schools run by parents, often in association with a religious group.
2. Schools organised by the government 'of origin' (e.g. Italian schools).
3. Local voluntary classes.

The Bullock Report of 1975 had included a chapter on the difficulties 'Children from families of overseas origin' faced with English, and had recommended that 'bilingual pupils should be encouraged to maintain their mother-tongues throughout their schooling'. Ten years later the Swann Report was the first attempt to respond systematically to the educational consequences of mass immigration, proposing the development of a 'pluralist' (i.e. not an assimilationist nor a separatist) society, openly advocating multiracial and multicultural education for all.

Local Authority educational practice was the subject of political controversy throughout the 1980s, as the Conservative Government moved towards centralising education, and the issue of multicultural and anti-racist education became a central area of dispute in the preparation of the 1988 Education Reform Act. In the 1990s, three themes seem to have emerged in the discussion of language rights:

1. The question of multiculturalism and anti-racism.
2. The recognition of other cultures across the National Curriculum.
3. Specific provision, either for language maintenance or for English as a Second Language.

Multiculturalism found little favour with the Conservative government, while anti-racist interventionism was – and is in 1996 – viewed with actual hostility. In the National Curriculum for English, introduced to schools in its final form from 1994, specific elements showing an awareness of other cultures were fairly rare, although it was hoped that pupils would read texts from other cultures. The history curriculum is, at the specific request of the Secretary of State, centred on Britain and British history. The actual provision of individual languages in schools can only realistically be measured by entries to GCSE, normally taken at age 16, which shows increases between 1988 and 1993 for all languages of some 28% over that period. French entries increased by 18.7%, German by 40.8%, the South-East Asian languages (Bengali, Hindi, Gujerati, Panjabi and Urdu) collectively increased by 99%, Arabic by 236%, Chinese by 150%. It would seem therefore, that provision for community languages is being taken up within the schools. Indeed, in the 1994 GCSE entries, Urdu, at 6,301, had more entries than Italian at 5,709, and was the fourth most popular foreign language. The politicisation of the question, together with uncertainty about the role of teachers, has not simplified the question. However, the National Curriculum Council commented that 'bilingualism is not, in itself, sufficient reason for disapplication of the National Curriculum. Although bilingual pupils often require language support, they are no more likely to have special educational needs than any other pupils'.

Germany

As a percentage of the population, immigrants have increased since 1960 when they accounted for 1.2 percent of the West German population. By 1970 they were over 4%, by 1990 8.4% and now form about 8% of reunified Germany, or some six and a half million people (Gogolin 1993; Horrocks and Kolinsky 1996). Immigrants to Germany fall into three groups: returning 'Germans' (Aussiedler), economic migrants and political refugees. The cultural background, even of the Aussiedler, has been determined by their life in other countries, even though they were regarded as a German minority there. Many do not speak German and few of them had schooling in German. Compared with the other groups of immigrants to contemporary Germany, they have special privileges: under no circumstances can they be threatened with expulsion, and they receive special social and psychological support that is intended to guarantee their rapid integration into the society of the Federal Republic. Nevertheless, they very often face hostility or racist attacks, just as the other groups of immigrants do.

The second group are economic immigrants, intended to stay for a short time and to be rapidly 'rotated', but were in fact encouraged to stay both by employers, for their skills, and unions, so that they could be integrated into reward systems. Non-German labour is about eight percent of both the labour force and, together with their families, of the total population. They represent the largest group among the immigrants in Germany. Most have lived twenty years or more in Germany and most of their children were born there. They do not intend to 'return'. The highest proportion (41% of the total in 1992) is Turks, followed by those from the former Yugoslavia (21%) and from Italy (12%), so immigrants in Germany do not mainly, at the moment, come from outside Europe. Nonetheless since many of the Turks are Muslim and there is increasing immigration from the Mediterranean countries generally, the situation is often perceived as one in which the ethnic minority is foreign both to German traditions and also to European ones.

The third group of immigrants, the one with least practical rights, is political asylum seekers. Less than 10% of applications for political asylum per year receive a positive answer, usually after long and time-consuming court cases. Indeed, only some 150,000 have been granted settlement rights since 1950, despite more than 2.5 million applications. Socially and demographically, Germany has been in considerable upheaval since 1945. The country had to absorb four million returning German prisoners of war between 1945 and 1950; twelve million people expelled from the East between 1945 and 1955; another 3.5 million Aussiedler between 1950 and 1995. Population losses from the Democratic to the Federal Republic amounted to 3.4 million between 1945 and 1961 and a further million until the Democratic Republic collapsed in 1989. The injection of six million foreign nationals to the labour market, has been followed by the strains consequent on the decision to reintegrate East and West as quickly as possible. Contemporary Germany is hence in considerable social turmoil, and policies and practices demonstrate at one and the same time features of a wish for inclusion and opposing tendencies towards exclusion.

Nearly 15% of school children belong to immigrant families. Immigrant children are the least successful in German schools. One of the reasons for this is the marginal status of their mother tongue in the German state school system, where progression from year to year is required. Non-speakers of German are often withdrawn from class and cannot attain the level of the others, and the extra coaching which many German eight-year-olds now receive is rarely available for them.

Overall, the migrant population became, after 1973, (considerably) younger and has stayed so: while a majority of the German population is aged forty and over, among non-Germans the proportion is nearer 30%. In terms of economic activity, too, the non-German minority is mainly blue-collar, and this pattern seems to be continuing for the second generation. Unemployment is more prevalent; housing is predominantly poor: 92% in rented accommodation, mainly in the larger cities; households are larger: for 30% of non-Germans, but 8% of Germans, they consist of four or more people. Perhaps more seriously, xenophobia and segregation are widespread, in both informal and minor ways – schoolchildren rarely mix – and in formal and more serious ones – opinion polls consistently show sixty percent of the population concerned about the 'foreigner problem', while murder, arson and hostile aggression have shown the strength of feeling. For one commentator at least 'For many Germans, exclusion remains an acceptable alternative' (Kolinsky in Horrocks and Kolinsky 1996, 104).

Holland

'The multi-ethnic, multicultural and multilingual nature of modern Dutch society (is) an issue of central importance in the Netherlands' (Kroon and Vallen 1994). On the basis that at least one parent was born outside Holland, about 15% of the present Dutch population are 'immigrants'. About half of these – 6.5 to 7% – about a million people – are commonly called ethnic minorities; about half of these come from the former Dutch colonies in Suriname, the Dutch Caribbean and Indonesia and the remainder from the Mediterranean fringe – Turkey, Morocco, and the former Yugoslavia. Government policies, like those in most of Europe, have concentrated on educational provision and generally have faced the same dilemmas: whether to separate children from ethnic minorities and make specific provision for them, or to ignore the differences and integrate and attempt to assimilate such children as quickly as possible. The analysis of the situation conducted in 1992 led to a number of conclusions and proposals for practical measures to cope with the situation in a Europe, where the increasing strength of right-wing opposition to special measures for ethnic minorities, and the increasing uncertainty of politicians in facing unemployment and growing financial difficulties, meant that the issue of official and unofficial migration could no longer be avoided.

The 1992 Van Kemenade Commission's conclusions sharpened thinking on three specific aspects of the Dutch policies: combating disadvantage; maintaining cultures and languages; and the involvement of immigrant families with the education of their children. The Commission took the view that the poor socio-economic position found in many ethnic groups was not, per se, any different from the poor socio-economic position of 'Dutch' children, and that therefore very similar procedures could be adopted for tackling the question of disadvantage. In the case of 'own languages' – where the stress was to be on language rather than on the associated culture – additional support was proposed for early bilingual teaching as a medium of instruction, followed by education in the standard language of ethnic groups in primary education. This was followed by the possibility of studying such a language – limited in the first instance to Turkish and Arabic – as an option in secondary education. Finally, the Commission took no clear view on family support, preferring to further develop an approach based on the provision of help through centres, rather than on identifying parental need.

These proposals did not altogether receive support among workers in the field, and it seems fairly clear that the basic dilemma between assimilation and pluralism has not been resolved and is unlikely to be further clarified by them. However, in many respects Dutch society, traditionally tolerant, has gone a lot farther than many European societies in accepting difference. Kroon and Vallen (1994, 125) exemplify both acceptance and rejection of ethnicity: while ritual slaughter of animals, in the Islamic tradition, is widely accepted and officially no longer a crime, the age of consent to marriage, and of compulsory education, remains at sixteen despite the widespread Islamic preference for the withdrawal of older daughters from public life.

Languages in contact

These examples of the contact between languages and cultures from within and from outside Europe, show that the political community is often in a difficult situation in its attempts to ensure social harmony. The fundamental issue is that of the recognition of difference, and of the policies and procedures which might be adopted to cope with the situation of most European countries: that migration towards them is often of large groups; that the previous colonial history of many countries remains present within their borders; and that obvious markers of difference – skin colour, language – are too often apt to become markers of social exclusion. Some countries have a long history of refusing to accept difference, and France in particular has become a unified and integrated society only by insisting on the creation and imposition of common identity which refuses 'particularisms'. Other traditionally open societies have found themselves facing situations of internal conflict, which are foreign to their open and welcoming nature. The next Chapter reviews some aspects of responses to these questions which are not often dealt with: the question of European language policy, the nature of language industries such as translation, and the role of artificial languages.

The dream of language harmony

Language, and the way we use it, is so closely bound up with our existence as human beings, both as individuals and as members of a community, that the subject arouses strong, even violent emotions. The indissoluble nature of the language-society link and the closeness of the use of language to expressions of identity are exemplified in the simple desire that everybody should have access to the standard language, and also in the violence of the Corsicans and the Basques opposing central authority, and the declarations of some States that everybody must use one language only. In every State, if not in every community, groups of people come constantly into contact with other groups equally determined to ensure that their identity, and their difference, is protected. To avoid conflict, there must be compromise or co-operation.

These three possible outcomes of language contact – conflict, compromise or co-operation – can be seen in different States and at different times. However, is there a better way of coping with the situation, than the various modes of living together that we have presented so far in this book? Is it possible for human beings and groups to live together in harmony through some other way than surrendering part of their own identity, or via some other mechanism than constant war, terrorist acts or domination, and its opposite, marginalisation? In essence there are only three possible solutions:

1. That individuals acquire another, common language, which they accept will be common to them all despite the emotional associations it necessarily has.
2. That individuals agree to use a common language which has no implications for their or anybody else's identity – either a language far removed from their everyday situation, or perhaps an artificial language.
3. That individuals learn more than one language, perhaps using one for one function or purpose and another for other domains of activity.

Each of these solutions can be immensely aided by translation, and by foreign language learning. All these solutions require the three types of community to understand their different roles, and particularly that a language policy be accepted by the political authorities, in much the same way that a foreign policy, or a social welfare policy, is accepted.

Why should a dream of language harmony be impossible? In theory it is not; there is no logical reason why a language policy should not be generally accepted. An *ipso facto* language policy has indeed been accepted by the many groups and individuals who have assimilated to dominant societies, or who have ensured that the political solution for them is to separate from the dominant group. Decisions on which foreign languages to learn at school reflect the language policy of the educational system. Support for translation, or for the language industries generally, whether provided by the State or by commercial interests, represent language planning. The history of Europe is full of examples of the absorption of massive immigration, of newly emergent nations, and of the reconstruction of nations, so the processes have worked – admittedly for better or worse – in the past. However, all these solutions assume language shift, that people move from one language to another, none of them is ideal and all have problems of different types.

This chapter briefly reviews three possible 'solutions' to Europe's language problems: the acceptance of a language policy on the political level; greater use of aids for the arduous task of translation or of 'interlanguage transfer'; and the use of an artificial language. There is just enough in each of these to make them tantalisingly possible, and to offer the prospect that impossible dreams may one day be realised.

A language policy for Europe?

The question of a possible language policy for the new European super-State which the European Community, and then the European Union, might turn into, has been discussed extensively in recent years (Coulmas 1991; Labrie 1993; Siguan 1996). If the new Europe is to be an integrated organisation, or so goes the argument, it will need to ensure that its member citizens can communicate freely. Like any other political State, this could be through designating one or more languages as official, or through a deliberate policy of multilingualism. Like any other State, too, the new Europe would need to define which foreign languages should be taught, whether every European child should have at least one language in common, how well they should know them and how many languages every schoolchild should learn. The main problem in all this, is to devise a policy which does not offend national susceptibilities – and hence simply accepting the *fait accompli* of English as the common European language is unlikely to be a deliberate policy for any member State. Britain is in a potentially awkward position, and the Foreign Office has a tradition of ensuring that it keeps out of the language question in order not to offend its neighbours – for what other policy could it possibly advance other than the obvious one that English should be required from all?

Historically, the question has become more complex as the Union has grown from its earliest beginnings as the Coal and Steel Community, into the European Community and eventually the European Union. In the first stages French was dominant while in the second stage, after Britain joined, a slow broadening of Union interests meant that English had to be used to communicate with the United States and international organisations like the United Nations. In the third stage of increasing and possibly continuous expansion, the simple practicalities of life have come to dominate the vastly increased international and world-wide activities of Commission and Council staff.

Multilingual States like India have come to accept a three-level policy:

1. A State or Federal language in which the State organisations operate and in which the State externalises itself.
2. A number of national languages which have such official status in their own territories – States, regions or provinces.
3. A larger number of regional (or non-territorial) languages which are used for specific and defined purposes (commerce, media, religion or for domestic purposes in a specific region or among a specified community).

Citizens can then choose to operate at regional, national or State level, or all of them, and will need to acquire the appropriate means of communication when they do so. Special language learning arrangements are made for Civil Servants, schoolchildren must learn the State language and can learn any number of national or regional languages; national education systems must provide teaching in at least the national languages. Individuals have both rights and duties: the right to use one of a number of specified languages, but also the duty to learn others for specific functions or at specific levels.

There are a number of different ways of tackling this question: from the linguistic point of view, the political, the economic, and from the cultural. But the basic question – what do we want a policy for – is rarely asked. It may be that a policy is required principally for the European institutions: what should be the language of the Parliament, the Commission, the Council of Ministers, the Courts of Justice? Is the policy needed so that any citizen can communicate practically with any other, in commercial or similar transactions? Or is a policy required to show friendship, fellow-feeling and a sense of Europeanness to all citizens? Is a policy required for now, or should it be limited to future generations and thus target particularly the educational institutions?

Once the purpose of a policy is decided, the 'how' of the question can be tackled: is there one language, natural or artificial, which is linguistically preferable to others? Does the solution lie in improved translation support, in interpreting, in the training of more linguistic 'go-betweens', rather than in attempting a blanket coverage of entire populations? Should one accept the practical situation and the majority vote, and if one does, does this mean basing a policy for a common language on the most widespread language in Europe, or the most widespread in the world? What are the lessons of language planning and policy decisions elsewhere? Is the Indian or the US model applicable to Europe, or is neither appropriate?

Questions such as these have been amply debated, but one can well object that any debate is theoretical, that in this area language planning and policy-making is merely an intellectual exercise and that it is the speech community that will eventually decide, as it does in the case of new terminology and at the level of any State. Against this view are the undeniable examples of Hebrew, where a long-dead language was given new life and became the official and popular language of a new State; and of Quebec, where a dying language was given new force and vitality from deliberate and sustained planning in the teeth of well-resourced, 'common-sense' and occasionally violent opposition.

Let us restrict discussion to three areas: a language for the European institutions; a lingua franca for all; and an educational policy for the future. The institutions currently spend enormous amounts of money on providing linguistic support: of the 1,700 administrative staff in the Commission, 1,200 were translators in the early 1990s producing nearly a million pages of translation annually. It would be financially advantageous if the translators and interpreters could be released, and the work of the institutions would be immensely improved if all participants could understand each other quickly. Realistically, the contenders are only French or English, and in practical terms, in preparatory meetings and often in the main meetings too, these are the only two that are used. Traditionally and historically, most institutions used French, as many international institutions still do; but English now outweighs French in this role and is used in the most recent institutions and in the most important areas – transport, finance and diplomacy. However, the French government is implacably opposed to a limitation to English only, and its reaction provokes similar blocking manoeuvres by other Governments. President Mitterrand's provocative letter of 1990 requesting that the institutions rigorously respect the role of French may have underlined the point. The Parliament has several times reaffirmed its support for a multilingual policy in its debates.

For European citizens as opposed to institutions, any one of the major European languages is of course a possibility as a lingua franca. A case can even be made, on linguistic grounds, for a revival of Latin. Yet among the natural languages, English, French and German are the only real contenders if one includes both linguistic and socio-political or economic considerations. What are the pros and cons for each of these? English has the enormous advantage of world use, but French is its predecessor in this role and is almost as widespread. German is the language of the greatest proportion of Europeans. English has the problem that it could be seen as a non-European language, since its main users lie outside the continent in the USA, Canada, Australia, India and New Zealand. French is undoubtedly a European language, but it is reputedly fairly difficult to learn and its defenders are said to hold an attitude which does not look kindly on its inefficient or uncertain use, and many European governments are suspicious that the enthusiastic defence of French by the French government, hides a strong desire to impose it and to dominate as English does currently. German provokes negative reactions among many who were dominated forty years ago, as indeed Russian does today among those in the East.

In education, the policy can only mean that the majority of children should learn one or more foreign languages. But which? Here, there is no doubt that the investment that has been made in teaching material by British and American publishers far outweighs that made by any other language, although the French and the Canadian governments have made significant investment also. At the European level, there have been funded initiatives by the European Commission itself through programmes such as LINGUA, COMETT and SOCRATES, mostly aimed at helping the exchange of students, whether of languages or other subjects, between schools and Universities. These programmes do not amount to a specific language policy, in that they respond to initiatives and must include three EU countries. Specific proposals have been made within the context of the French Governments 'multilingual initiative' during its 1995 Presidency of the Union, that member countries should actively pursue a policy of teaching two foreign languages for all in education – English plus one other – but to ensure that English children also learned two European languages – the hope being that in any group of Europeans there would always be the possibility of mutual comprehension in at least one European language. However, the policy was not fully adopted.

The main problem with language planning for Europe is that there is no organisation which could come to conclusions and implement a policy:

- While France has a range of language organisations, Britain has none.
- The European Parliament for the moment is a talking shop with no executive powers.
- The Council of Ministers – presumably of Culture, since there are no Ministers for Language – sees the problem as of less than immediate urgency.
- The Commission, the European executive, has no Commissioner charged with this responsibility and indeed it is doubtful whether the founding Treaties provide any ground for assuming that a common European policy will emerge.

Again, since language and society are interlinked, Eurosceptics wherever they are, see this field as a red rag to a bull. For the moment, the issue remains either an intriguing area of debate or is rapidly avoided.

The language industries and language engineering

Another solution to Europe's language problem might lie in the improvement of interlanguage communication. With modern computers, improved and much more rapid translation and interpreting, the wide availability of linguistic support, the language barrier might be overcome. Possible technological solutions are many and varied, and the 'language industries' and the concept of 'language engineering' have grown up to put them into effect. One of the best developed of such schemes is the use of computers in translation.

Machine translation

Translation is difficult, and in the view of some experts, impossible, because language never labels an abstract external reality, but imposes on the external world a particular way of seeing it. Translating from one language to another is nonetheless a widespread activity in a large number of fields. The translation industry in most European countries is large, poorly organised, dependent on a large number of unskilled or semi-skilled workers – typically earning very small amounts – and without any overall legal or professional control, certification or indeed approvals mechanism. In some limited domains – the law, some contractual fields – translators are certified and do take legal responsibility for what they write. In most, the rule is that the buyer has to beware.

However, with the possible exception of translating film dialogue, translation is required much less in the more difficult areas of language use – poetry, imaginative writing – than in the more mundane fields of the scientific and commercial world, where what is needed is in effect, the relabelling of international concepts. In fields like these, translation is fairly mechanical, the same words and phrases recur with monotonous frequency, they are (nearly) always translated the same way, and there is no reason why much of the drudgery should not be done by mechanical means, automatically translating the same words and phrases by looking up the same equivalent as was used before, every time they are met. Machine translation could apparently do the job efficiently.

In the early days there was a widespread belief that all translation was merely a matter of recoding. Russian, for example, was 'really' English only expressed in a different code, and translation was a matter of substitution. The next stage, when it was realised that language was much more complex than this, was to compare a pair of languages, by analysing the systems and vocabulary of language A and transferring as directly as possible from these to the systems and vocabulary of language B. The most efficient system must however be one in which the machine translates first to an abstract or artificial language, so that it can then output from this abstact set of concepts to any natural language. The difficulties of actually doing this in practice however, mean that it has not yet been implemented and the most successful systems still operate at the craft level of comparing language pairs more or less directly. One of the most successful machine translation systems is Systran, originally developed in the United States and used by organisations in the European Community from 1975 (L'Huillier 1990). The system has grown by adding to its own capacities and techniques, so it is anything but a tidy system in computer terms. However, it seems to work, despite, in its early stages, being prone to fairly obvious mistranslations like La Cour de Justice envisage la création d'un cinquième poste d'avocat général translated as The yard of justice is considering the creation of a fifth general avocado station.

Computerisation: the information revolution

Modern computers are far removed from the massive number-crunchers of earlier generations, whose purpose was to add up, multiply and divide numerical data for banks, the defence industry and scientific research. Today, it is generally accepted that the usefulness of computers lies in their ability to handle enormous quantities of symbolic data, such as language. Computers can deal with much of the complexity of natural languages, disseminate their information widely and can ensure that linguistic information is associated with graphic, numerical or symbolic data as well, as anybody with experience of computer games, the Internet or computer graphics can testify. Communication between those who do not have a language in common could thus use such non-language interfaces – diagrams, sketches, still and moving images – that could at least help to clarify discussion; in some areas, such as the international comparison of architectural drawings, statistical evaluation or aesthetic assessment, they could replace much verbiage.

Computerisation: support for language users

One of the most effective ways in which computer power has been used is however, by recognising the limitations of computers and accepting them. This approach starts from the belief that human translators or language users will always be more flexible than any machine, and that therefore what the machine can do best is to provide the human with support for the difficult aspects by making the simple parts easier and quicker. Surely, it is said, if translation actually does take place, as it certainly does, then the massive data-handling capacities of computers must be able to ensure that every possibility is presented to the translator, in the same way that every possibility can be analysed in chess, and the human translator can then choose the most appropriate. Machine terminologies can provide accurate descriptions of what a term means through a definition, can give access to examples of the use of a term in the context of a phrase, a paragraph or a whole text, can give a list of synonyms and similar words with all the detail about how they have been used in sample texts. Such a terminology bank in one language can be associated with a similar one in another language, through a bilingual bank of terms, and one can thus compare how the term is used in one language with how it is used in another. What is more, the information can be made available much faster than a bilingual dictionary and can be flexibly used to enable searching through a mass of data in order to provide the best possible help for the writer or translator, in the task of selecting the eventual item they need.

Artificial languages

The third 'solution' to Europe's language problems lies in the use of an artificial language. Several hundred attempts have been made at inventing artificial languages. Artificial languages, precisely because they are artificial, have no social or political associations, so they should be acceptable to all. Their widespread use would mean that all Europe's dwellers – and indeed all humanity – would have access to the whole of human knowledge.

One of the most successful artificial languages is Esperanto. Esperanto was invented in Poland in 1887 by Ludwig Lazarus Zamenhof, an oculist and later Government employee. It soon achieved greater success than its immediate predecessor, Volapük, and is now perhaps the most widespread international language[1]. Zamenhof aimed at creating an international language which could be accepted by all nations and be the property of the whole world, without belonging to any existing nationality. He considered that three problems needed to be solved for his artificial language to be successful: the language should be easy to learn; it had to be viable from the outset for international communication, and, somehow, the indifference of the bulk of mankind should be overcome so that use of Esperanto would not require constant use of a dictionary and should be as natural as possible. The Fundamento de Esperanto, published in 1905 contained the sixteen original rules devised in 1887, a vocabulary of 1,800 roots and examples of use. It has remained as a sort of holy Bible for Esperantists since, enabling them to withstand possible changes such as those proposed in the 'Ido Schism' of 1908, in which a development of Esperanto nearly succeeded in replacing it.

Esperanto's sixteen rules try to ensure that every aspect of the language is as regular as possible. Stress always falls on the penultimate syllable; one letter represents one sound and there are no silent letters, although there exist a number of letters with circumflexes or followed by the letter h – e.g. sh, pronounced as in show. There is one invariable definite article la; nouns always end in -o, adjectives in -a; verb forms are invariable for person and change for tense: mi faras, I do, li faris, he did, ili faros, they will do. Most vocabulary is based on Latin – akvo water, tero earth – while other words are easily recognisable in many European languages – birdo bird, kato cat. Esperanto has a system of agreement: bona hundo (good dog), bonaj hundoj (good dogs); and of word-building, by which prefixes and suffixes have specific meanings and a word like malsanulejo (hospital), for example, can be constructed from mal- (opposite), sana (health), -ul (person characterised by the idea in the root), -ej (place) and -o (noun).

Criticisms have been made of the rules and their results: malsanulejo is hardly an obvious word for hospital, and there is little logic in deciding that malbela (ugly: 'unbeautiful') is any more appropriate than a form like 'unugly' would be; much vocabulary has been created which foxes English, French or German users (foresta – absent). Basing the language on European vocabulary, spelling and European linguistic systems makes it difficult for Asian and other learners unaccustomed to Roman script and European language systems.

Many schools and universities have used and taught Esperanto; it is part of available curricula in many countries although, only rarely a required element. The language has many supporters working in international organisations, and the early meetings of the League of Nations commissioned reports to see whether it might be used as a means of communication for the organisation. The Third Assembly, meeting in Geneva in 1922, decided not. Esperanto has been used, not merely for translations from natural languages, but also as a language of original literary creation. Similarly, there are cases of children who have been brought up using Esperanto as their mother tongue.

Why was Esperanto successful where predecessors and indeed followers have not proved so popular? One of the major reasons must be the deliberate choice of its inventor not to claim it as his sole property in the early stages, and to ensure that a community of Esperantists was created early on. In fact, by 1893 there was already a group of subscribers to La Esperantisto who could act as referees for any changes proposed, and who did very shortly vote for leaving the language more or less unchanged, as Zamenhof had invented it. Esperanto quickly spread outside the Russian Poland where it had been invented, and gained support from France, which hosted the First Universal Congress in 1905 in Boulogne, and from Britain. At this First Congress Zamenhof gave up any personal rights to the language, declared that the only fundamental rule for Esperantists was that they must accept the Fundamento, and said in clear terms that the only purpose of the language was to spread the use of a neutral language which would provide a means of mutual understanding.

What are the arguments for or against an artificial language? In favour, of course, must be the lack of association with a specific social or political community. Secondly, communication on science or commerce should be facilitated by the use of an artificial language, in which concepts would be common to scientists or businessmen of any community. Early attempts at artificial languages were often motivated by a belief that rational thinking would be helped by avoiding all the ambiguities and complexities of natural languages. A philosophical or rational language would enable all clear-thinking people – usually men – to communicate in a completely unbiased way. An artificial language should be easy to learn.

However, artificial languages are never completely artificial. In order to make them learnable they must have some recognisable components, and most have developed a vocabulary and a grammatical system based on European languages. So what they have done is, in effect, to simplify reality rather than reconceptualise it. But the more their origins are transparent and thus easy for European learners, the more difficult they are for non-Europeans. Secondly, their advantages are also their defects: artificial languages must have rigid, unbreakable rules and yet the whole point of language is that if it is to represent changing human reality it must be able itself to change to a certain extent. Similarly, one of the problems with translation is that the words in any language represent the reality of the political or social community using it. Since by definition Esperanto has no social or political community its words can either represent any community or none: words like democracy, President, Parliament can mean anything or nothing. Scientific concepts might be conveyed by Esperanto, but since scientific concepts are created within a linguistic environment 'Esperanto science' is inconceivable, whereas French mathematics or Russian biochemistry is possible. Generally speaking, there are few serious linguists or politicians who think that an artificial language can solve Europe's language planning problem.

Europe, the Community and the State: the future.

It is always difficult to predict the future. It is even more difficult to predict it correctly. This section will hence be a complete hostage to fortune, even though one can be fairly sure that uncertainty will prevail.

It is fairly unlikely that language-related questions will subside in importance. The ferocity of the emotions bound up with questions of identity, with the symbolic nature of language as a representative of that identity, and with the role of identity in the presentation of questions of politics, economics and society, means that one can predict with certainty, that any community's representatives will continue to see language as a symbol of their identity, and try to match its role with the role they desire for themselves and their community.

It is also fairly clear that the main principles on which communities operate, will continue to lead to identifiable results not much different from those we see in operation today. Some socially or economically insecure communities will shift from one language or language variety to another, and this will particularly affect migrants from southern to northern Europe and economically insecure groups like those speaking Rhaeto-Romansh. Well established language communities – and particularly those with previously fairly secure political backing in independent States – will increasingly defend their language or variety from what they see as attacks on it, particularly if these come, in their view, from outside Europe: not solely the French, but also and increasingly Germany, although such actions may not be shared by the other German-speaking countries. Others – Britain is the prime example – will affect not to be aware of the existence of the language dimension in what they do, but will be forced by increasing nationalism elsewhere in Europe to take practical steps to support their language, whether in spreading its use abroad or in defending 'correct usage' at home. There is yet some way to go for the present ferocity of national and ethnic feeling to subside, and yet more vicious wars to be fought on this issue as Europe continues to readapt from the collapse of the Eastern Empire.

Most immigrant communities, particularly those from North Africa and the Middle East in France or Germany, will slowly adopt the host language and eventually assimilate to their new home. Some immigrant groups – Asians in Britain, Turks in Germany – will develop a mixed culture which is neither that of their Asian origin nor that of the host country. They will possibly develop, too, a mixed language recognisably different from that of the host country, because they retain strong connections with both sending and receiving countries, and undertake constant and renewed travel and both they and their children have prolonged stays in both countries. France will insist on the cultural exception from any internationalisation, particularly if this means accepting the influence of any power other than itself, and will insist on retaining its own uniqueness, trying to force Europe to model itself on the French perception of the Nation-State. Germany will continue to use its economic strength to retain its identity, but will not associate this closely with the retention of any one dialect of German nor even of German as a means of communication: it may go so far as to sacrifice culture for economic advantage. Britain will affect to ignore the existence of language-related questions for so long as English retains a strong international role and Britain can shelter behind the United States. Europe generally will move only very slowly to greater integration, whether on the economic, political or social front, and indeed as the social and cultural realities of forced economic integration are realised, may deliberately weaken the latter.

This fairly bleak picture can of course be alleviated. The present identity-related conflictual scene could be modified by greater understanding of others through increased learning of foreign languages, more travel and closer contact, and the greater internationalisation and globalisation of existing contacts, particularly commercial ones. Europe's language policies, particularly in education, could ensure that foreign languages are widely taught and widely used. However, Europe generally will have to wait until the consequences of the break-up of the Soviet Union are absorbed, and until the social effects of the Maastricht convergence within the European Union are made clear. While present barriers between languages and cultures may nor retain their previous impermeability, it will be some time yet before Europe may lay claim to its own identity through its own freely chosen, freely used and widely understood language.

References

Ager, D. E. Sociolinguistics and Contemporary French. Cambridge University Press: Cambridge, 1990.

Ager, D. E. Language learning and European integration. In Beveridge, M. and Reddiford, G. (eds). Language, culture and education. Multilingual Matters: Clevedon, 1993, 68-83.

Ager, D. E. Immigration and language policy in France. Journal of Intercultural Studies, 1995, 15, 2: 35-52.

Ager, D. E. Francophonie in the 1990s. Problems and Opportunities. Multilingual Matters: Clevedon, 1996a.

Ager, D. E. Identity, insecurity and image: the objectives of language policy in France and the Francophone world. University of Surrey: Conference on French language policies, June 1996b.

Ager, D. E. Language policy in Britain and France. The processes of policy. Cassell Academic: London, 1996c.

Ager, D. E., Muskens, G. and Wright, S. (eds) Language Education for Interlingual Communication. Multilingual Matters: Clevedon, 1993.

Ball, M. J. (ed) The Celtic languages. Routledge: London, 1993.

Baugh, A. C. and Cable, T. A history of the English language. Prentice-Hall: Englewood Cliffs, New Jersey, 3rd edition 1978.

Baxter, A. Portuguese as a pluricentric language. In Clyne, M. (ed) Pluricentric languages. Differing norms in different nations. Berlin: Mouton de Gruyter: Berlin, 1992, 11-43.

Beheydt, L. The linguistic situation in the new Belgium. Current issues in language and society, 1994, 1, 2: 147-63.

Beveridge, M. and Reddiford, G. (eds) Language, culture and education. Multilingual Matters: Clevedon, 1993.

Burchfield, R. (ed) The Cambridge History of the English Language. Volume V English in Britain and Overseas. Cambridge University Press: Cambridge, 1994.

Calvet, J.-L. L'Europe et ses langues. Plon: Paris, 1993.

Chansou, M. Evaluation d'une action de politique linguistique. Les travaux de la Commission ministérielle de terminologie de l'audiovisuel et de la publicité. Terminologies nouvelles, 1994, 12: 107-113.

Clyne, M. The German language in a changing Europe. Cambridge University Press: Cambridge, 1996.

Clyne, M. (ed) Pluricentric languages. Differing norms in different nations. Mouton de Gruyter: Berlin, 1992.

Comrie, B. Russian. In Comrie, B. (ed). The World's Major Languages. Croom Helm: London, 1987, 329-47.

Comrie, B (ed). The World's Major Languages. Croom Helm: London, 1987.

Comrie, B. and Stone, G. The Russian language since the Revolution. Clarendon Press: Oxford, 1978.

Corbett, G. Serbo-Croat. In Comrie, B (ed) The World's Major Languages. Croom Helm: London, 1987, 391-409.

Coulmas, F. Language and Economy. Blackwell: Oxford, 1992.

Coulmas, F. (ed) A language policy for the European Community: prospects and quandaries. Mouton de Gruyter: Berlin, 1991.

Crystal, D. The Cambridge Encyclopedia of language. Cambridge University Press: Cambridge, 1987.

Edwards, J. Multingualism. Routledge: London, 1996.

Entwistle, W. J. The Spanish Language. Faber and Faber: London, 2nd edition 1962.

Fernandez-Armesto, F. (ed) The Times Guide to the Peoples of Europe. Times Books: London, 1994.

Garvin, P.L. A conceptual framework for the study of language standardisation. International Journal of the Sociology of Language, 1993, 100/101: 37-54.

Giordan, H. (ed) Les Minorités en Europe. Editions Kimé: Paris, 1992.

Gogolin, I. Multilingualism in the German school. In Ager, D. E., Muskens, G. and Wright, S. (eds) Language Education for Interlingual Communication. Multilingual Matters: Clevedon, 1993, 91-107.

Green, J. Spanish. In Comrie, B (ed). The World's Major Languages. Croom Helm: London, 1987, 236-59.

Grillo, R. D. Dominant languages. Language and hierarchy in Britain and France. Cambridge University Press: Cambridge, 1989.

Guillorel, H. La politique entre la purification et le laisser-aller linguistiques. In Eloy, J.-M. (ed) La Qualité de la langue. Champion: Paris, 1995, 327-65.

Hagège, C. Le souffle de la langue. Odile Jacob: Paris, 1992.

Hamers, J. F. and Blanc, M. Bilinguality and bilingualism. Cambridge University Press: Cambridge, 1989.

Harris, M. French. In Comrie, B. (ed) The World's Major Languages. Croom Helm: London, 1987, 210-35.

Haugen, E. The Scandinavian languages. Faber and Faber: London, 1976.

Hawkins, J. A. German. In Comrie, B. (ed) The World's Major Languages. Croom Helm: London, 1987, 110-38.

Horrocks, D. and Kolinsky, E. Turkish Culture in German Society Today. Berghahn Books: Providence and Oxford, 1996.

Istituto della Enciclopedia Italiana. Les Minorités Linguistiques dans les pays de la Communauté Européenne. Office des Publications Officielles des Communautés Européennees: Luxembourg, 1986.

Jones, R. O. The sociolinguistics of Welsh. In Ball, M. J. (ed) The Celtic languages. Routledge: London, (1993), 536-605.

Kellas, J. G. The politics of nationalism and ethnicity. Macmillan: London, 1991.

Keller, R. E. The German Language. Humanities Press Inc.: New Jersey, 1978.

Knowles, F. E. From USSR to CIS and beyond: visceral politics vis-à-vis ethno-linguistic realities. In Ager, D. E., Muskens, G. and Wright, S. (eds) Language Education for Interlingual Communication. Multilingual Matters: Clevedon, 1993, 131-58.

König, E. and van der Auwera, J. (eds) The Germanic languages. Routledge: London, 1994.

Kroon, S. and Vallen, T. Multilingualism and education: an overview of language and education policies for ethnic minorities in the Netherlands. Current Issues in language and society, 1994, 1, 2: 103-29.

Labrie, N. La construction linguistique de la Communauté Européenne. Henri Champion: Paris, 1993.

Large, A. The Artificial Language Movement. Basil Blackwell: Oxford, 1985.

L'Huillier, M. Machine and human translation. In Fawcett P. and Heathcote O. (eds) Translation in Performance. Bradford Occasional Papers. Department of Modern Languages, University of Bradford: Bradford, 1990, 10: 61-85.

Liégeois, J.-P. Les Tsiganes: situation d'une minorité non-territoriale. In Giordan, H. (ed). Les Minorités en Europe. Editions Kimé: Paris, 1992, 417-43.

Lodge, R. A. French from dialect to standard. Routledge: London, 1993.

Migliorini, B. and Gwynfor Griffith, T. (1984). The Italian Language. Faber and Faber: London, First editions 1960, 1966.

Noreiko, S. New words for new technologies. In Sanders, C. (ed) French today. Cambridge University Press: Cambridge, 1993, 171-84.

Parry, M. M., Davies, W. W. and Temple, R. A. M. The Changing voices of Europe. Social and political changes and their linguistic repercussions, past, present and future. University of Wales Press: Cardiff, 1994.

Phillipson, R. Linguistic Imperialism. Oxford University Press: Oxford, 1992.

Ruhlen, M. A Guide to the world's languages. Vol 1: Classification. Stanford University Press: Stanford, 1987.

Sanders, C. (ed). French today. Cambridge University Press: Cambridge, 1993.

Shelley, M., Winck, M. (eds) Aspects of European Cultural Diversity. Volume 2 of the Second Level Open University Course 'What is Europe?'. Routledge: London, 1993.

Siguan, M. L'Europe des langues. Mardaga: Sprimont, 1996.

Truchot, C. (ed). Le plurilinguisme européen. Honoré Champion: Paris, 1994.

Trudgill, P. The social differentiation of English in Norwich. Cambridge University Press: Cambridge, 1974.

Vilfan, S. (ed) Ethnic groups and language rights. European Science Foundation. New York: New York University Press and Dartmouth Press: Aldershot, 1993.

Zetterholm, S. (ed) National cultures and European integration. Exploratory essays on cultural diversity and common policies. Berg: Providence and Oxford, 1994.

intellect

EUROPEAN STUDIES SERIES

General Editor: *Keith Cameron*

Available now

Humour and History	Keith Cameron (ed)
The Nation: Myth or Reality?	Keith Cameron (ed)
Regionalism in Europe	Peter Wagstaff (ed)
Women in European Theatre	Elizabeth Woodrough (ed)
Children and Propaganda	Judith Proud
The New Russia	Michael Pursglove(ed)
English Language in Europe	Reinhard Hartmann (ed)
Food in European Literature	John Wilkins (ed)
Theatre and Europe	Christopher McCullough
European Identity in Cinema	Wendy Everett (ed)
Television in Europe	James A. Coleman & Brigitte Rollet (eds)
Women Voice Men	Maya Slater (ed)

Published in 1998

Policing in Europe	Bill Tupman